"Call Me Dad, Not Dude"

"Call Me Dad, Not Dude"

◆

Humorous Commentaries on Parenting and Coping in Today's World

A collection of Matthew Keenan's best columns, published in The Kansas ity Star 2000–2007

Matthew D. Keenan

iUniverse, Inc.
New York Lincoln Shanghai

“Call Me Dad, Not Dude”
Humorous Commentaries on Parenting and Coping in Today’s World

iUniverse books may be ordered through booksellers or by contacting:

iUniverse
2021 Pine Lake Road, Suite 100
Lincoln, NE 68512
www.iuniverse.com
1-800-Authors (1-800-288-4677)

ISBN: 978-0-595-43851-8 (pbk)
ISBN: 978-0-595-88176-5 (ebk)

Printed in the United States of America

I dedicate this book to the one person who encouraged and inspired me to pursue my dream. My wife, Lori.

I owe my contributing columnist position to one Michael (O.J.) Nelson, Assistant Managing Editor, Kansas City Star. O.J. placed his confidence in me some seven years ago when no one else would. Along the way, others were very helpful, including my wife Lori, my two brothers Tim and Marty, my two sisters, Kate and Beth, my parents, my editors at the paper, Jeff Gerber, John Collar, Kris Knowles, and my current editor, Michelle Tevis. And of course, the readers of the Star, who have supported me over the years.

Contents

1

Raising Teenagers—God Help Us All

I am an imperfect parent. I am an imperfect husband. But along the way, our family has avoided major disasters that beset some families. I count that to luck as much as anything, plus a collection of Guardian Angels that work overtime. Here are my best columns on parenting.

Attention parents, beware of the Axe in the air

Teenagers these days are into image. At least mine are. That's a good thing, I suppose. But every once in a while their fashion demands conflict with my definition of reality. That tends to be a bad thing.

About two months ago, I was rounding up the boys for school. It was 7:30. My wife and I had to wake them, feed them, brush their teeth, load up their backpacks, toss them in the car (pillow optional), complete homework assignments and wake them up again just before we pushed them out the door and into the parking lot—all in about 15 minutes.

My sons' bedroom—roughly the size of a phone booth—had its door shut. When I opened it, I couldn't breathe or see. A fog was circulating around my eighth- and sixth-grade sons as they finished dressing. It was cloud-like. But there was no mistaking heaven here. This cloud smelled. When I questioned son two, he said, "Dude! It's Axe. Chill out." Axe, my wife explained, is what they call a "deodorant and body spray."

Deodorant I got no problem with, but body spray? So now their bedroom, the hallway and substantial parts of the living room have been "axed." And our home is not alone. A couple months ago, The Wall Street Journal had an article about Axe on the front page, above the fold, describing another cultural fad that is red-hot for the next couple months and then will fade. No problem, except in the meantime I need to breathe.

The level of application, as best I can tell, is inverse to age. My youngest drips in it. And because his aim has been horrible dating back to when he was potty-trained, his errant shots explain the rolling morning fog. Parents constantly fight the latest fads. My wife and I have prevailed on many—bleaching the hair, $100 basketball shoes, Under Armour (clothing), laser pointers, gas-powered scooters, to name just a couple. But this one got by us somehow.

The Journal noted that "teen fashion has veered away from grunge and hip-hop looks and toward preppy, clean cut attire that lends itself to more fastidious grooming." Axe comes in various "flavors": Touch, Essence and Phoenix are just three. The packaging says "Essence is an energetic, seductive and masculine fragrance."

My worry list is long these days. But teenagers named Keenan being seductive ain't on it.

The packaging talks about the Axe effect, which means girls chasing your son down the school hallway—provided they have a head cold. In our home we have our own Axe effects: windows opening and the gag reflex.

Axe can clear out a room faster than piano practice. In the '70s we had cologne. No one dared to use the words "body" and "spray" in the same sentence. Brut was big, but my dad liked Hai Karate. As kids we would sneak in his bedroom, apply it liberally and then run around the house screaming "Hi ya!" while karate-chopping my kid sister.

The late '70s brought Polo. The big city boys in my fraternity loved that stuff. These were the guys who had things I did not: Top-Siders, Izod shirts, money, cars, girlfriends—a life, basically. They used Polo liberally. One of my frat brothers from Mission Hills had a name for his Polo, a word that no family paper would ever print. When he would go "out on the town" you could smell him all the way from the Wheel, a popular student hangout. Last I heard, he was still a bachelor.

So Axe, for the time being, is here to stay. And if you are a parent of a teenage boy, you know the fog. So do something that we have attempted—unsuccessfully. Point out to your son the fine print in the packaging: "Avoid excessive inhalation."

Published January 22, 2005

Ten rules for finding lost shoes

Children have no short-term memory. Every parent knows this. They can never remember anything they did five hours ago or even five minutes ago. Never is this more true than when your son or daughter needs to locate the shoes that were kicked off moments earlier. They will never remember and often won't even try.

So out of this parental frustration I've carved in sandstone The Ten Commandments of Lost Shoes. And with the return of school, these are rules every parent needs to know.

1. It's the parent's fault they are lost. Don't argue the point. It wastes valuable time. Your child is too busy misplacing something else important. Start looking.

2. Ignore logic and common sense. The shoes are never, ever where they should be. Forget looking near the front door, front porch, in his closet, bedroom, or backseat of the car. That's too obvious. Never been there, never going there.

3. Where one shoe is found, the other is nowhere close. It's not in the same room, not in the same county. Shoes grow legs and walk—no, run—into different parts of the house. It happens every night. One of life's mysteries. Accept it. Don't attempt to understand it. You have no time for such things. You are late and growing later. Your child, of course, could care less.

4. Soccer shoes are the hardest to find. These shoes have cleats in some unique formation that some soccer geek decided can be used only for soccer. Consequently, these shoes have no real useful purpose, other than to play soccer, which really doesn't count. Next come baseball shoes, then basketball shoes, followed by any shoes your son needs to wear to church. These are all in a special class of shoes that can hide for months at a time.

5. **Don't ask questions.** Asking your son or daughter, "Where did you take them off?" will extend the search by five minutes every time you ask. Same with "Where did you leave them?" Yelling at them only prolongs the agony. Blaming your spouse reduces the size of the search party. Remain calm. Exhale.

6. **Start times.** The closer you are to the event starting, the higher the probability of not finding it in time. 'Nuf said.

7. **Wrong Shoe.** When you think you found them, they belong to another sibling. If the pair belongs to the right child, he's outgrown them. For your daughters, it's the pair that doesn't match the dress. Keep looking.

8. **Video Games.** Always check near the video game console. There is something about kids and video games. The first thing they do is take off their shoes. It helps them reach a new high score. That's what my son told me once. Next, check under blankets, pillows, sleeping bags and between the empty sacks of Doritos sitting next to the console. You are getting close to jackpot and the soccer game starts in two minutes.

9. **There is always something else.** Once you find them, and they fit, there is something else missing. Think fast. Most likely suspects: shin guards, batting gloves or water bottles.

10. **Mark the Spot.** Wherever you eventually find them, mark the spot. That location is where you will find the Blockbuster video rental that's two weeks past due, the library book checked out in 1997 and the spelling list your son misplaced in 1995. And when you find these, grab them now. Because 10 minutes later they have moved—to some other obscure location you will next find in 2005.

So it's Saturday morning, and your child's game begins in just two hours. His shoes—whether you know it or not—are missing. So start at the top of my 10 rules and work your way down. If you begin now, you'll make the second half.

Published October 22, 2003

Now appearing at your street corner: the orthodontist

In today's culture, every adolescent falls into one of two categories: They've either had braces on their teeth or will get them. Guaranteed. Two of my sons were born with straight teeth. No matter. They got braces. Now their teeth are truly perfect, and I'm broke.

Orthodontia is now a boom industry. Just look around. Their offices are more plentiful than the golden arches. They are in strip malls, on pricey street corners and have taken over all the prime spots south of 135th Street.

All of this comes with a substantial price tag. Orthodontists have a solution for this, of course. They offer elaborate plans of financing with multipage contracts. You sign it in triplicate in four different places. Car leases are more understandable. They offer payment plans over five to 10 years. When your son gets his college diploma, you've paid the bill in full.

Let me be clear, however. I like my son's orthodontists. It's a husband and wife team. They are masters at beautiful teeth. Their office is a cross between the pediatrician and a hair salon operated by a loan officer. It's a highly efficient operation.

Your appointment begins with a phone call—from a computer reminding you of the appointment. When you arrive, the waiting room is filled with patients. Average age: 11. The magazine rack features Highlights, Gameboy Today and Power Rangers Illustrated.

Eventually your son will take a seat in a line with similarly aged patients and wait as the doctors move down the line to adjust, pull and manipulate the wires. For every doctor there are nine assistants. They are drones the doctors purchased at some orthodontist convention in Malibu.

This year my seventh-grade son gets his braces off. Then we can start life with a thing called a retainer. In Spanish the word retainer means "lost."

The only family member who can consistently find our retainer is Bernie. The dog. And when he is finished with it, it's back to you know where.

I am not used to any of this. In western Kansas most parents couldn't spell orthodontist, let alone hire one. My hometown was lucky to have a dentist. Childhood imperfections were a part of life. And crooked teeth were part of being a kid. Every neighborhood had kids with teeth that were either buck, chipped or just dead. It was like a birthmark. Dental malformations were how you could tell the kids apart.

I can't tell you how many times around the dinner table my dad would ask:
"Now which friend is that?"
"Dad, he's got the chipped front tooth."
"Upper or lower?"
"Lower."
"Sure. Nice kid."

Back then the parents who demanded perfection in their children made them endure torture worthy of the Hussein brothers. We had an orthodontist who drove to Great Bend one day a week from Hutchinson. Ninety-nine percent of his patients were girls. The wiring on their teeth was thicker than bridge cable. His patients' mouths had more metal than most Buicks. My older sister Kate got braces. She would get food stuck between the metallic bands that a high powered water hose couldn't dislodge. It was disgusting. And her breath could gas out a small army.

Her braces included huge springs like a trampoline across her front teeth. At night she wore more head gear than a hockey goalie. She plastered her face in Clearasil, with her hair wrapped around orange cans (It's true—ask my brothers!) It put her in a very bad mood. And living with three brothers did nothing to improve her disposition. She was the devil, I'm pretty sure. But you should see her teeth now. Absolutely perfect.

So things have changed a lot in 30 years. Braces are everywhere. Even Tom Cruise got them. That hasn't helped me understand any of his movies, however. So if you see my sons, please make them smile. And ask them to hold it for a long time. I need to get my money's worth.

Published April, 2004

High School Prom Productions Big and Getting Bigger

Something quite unusual is going on in Johnson county right now. I have noticed it every Saturday night for the last couple weeks. It's the appearance of a fleet of limousines driving around our neighborhoods. Initially, I assumed they were rock stars trying to find Kemper Arena. And then someone explained to me that the prospective passengers were far more important than a high priced musician. They were dates to the High School Prom.

In my hometown in western Kansas, late 70's, Prom was a big deal too. My classmates and I sported the finest suits you could manufacture from petroleum by-products. Lapels wide enough to land a Jumbo Jet. The suits were quite 'leisurely'. Collars were wide open. Chest hair was appropriately coifed and curled. The look was a combination between Daniel Boone and Austin Powers. And our dates—and their dresses—well, I frankly don't remember much about those. It was guys night out. At the mature age of 17, we were completely confident that we knew everything about anything. Looking back, we were the biggest losers ever to sport a boutonniere and pose for a picture.

Today, I'm reliably told, the passage of twenty five years has not made Prom any less of a spectacle. Stretch limos are just the beginning. You have shoes, hair, nails, and earrings. But enough of the boys. For the girls, weddings come cheaper. In terms of parental planning, it is the adolescent equivalent of "Father of the Bride." Only the mothers have a say; fathers are advised to clear out and keep their mouths shut. Many weeks of marital discord are promised if the dad utters such comments as 'geez, it's just one night' or 'Oh come on—she's just a junior in high school'. And a frost will come over the bedspread if you dare state the obvious: 'haven't we exceeded our budget for this activity?'

The primary rules for the dress purchase are that it 1) cost a fortune; 2). look tasteful while covering as little as possible; and 3). cost a fortune. Other essentials include acquiring the perfect tan to match the pedicures, manicures, facials. Makeup is to applied, then subjected to massive tearing, and then reapplied repeatedly.

All of this work is then memorialized in a photo shoot that would make the Ford Modeling Agency blush. The dates frequently meet at one location. The room is a beehive of activity. The girls are preening and looking beautiful. The mothers are tinkering and cooing. The fathers are standing in the corner, looking at their watches, wondering how much it is going to cost to develop all of the film. The smart ones keep these thoughts to themselves. The brilliant ones participate in this process, to the icy stares of their uninvolved colleagues.

I thought the Keenans led a complicated existence. I was wrong. Because my kids are at least 5 years away from this unique form of parental stress, my wife and I can relax, be entertained by these stories, and provide directions to the lost limo drivers in our neighborhood. But I suspect these days as an amused observer are growing shorter. Right now, it's a major production for my daughter Maggie to decide on her dress, bow, and then shoes on any given day. I cannot imagine what awaits me when Guido, her date, is perched on our porch, impatiently pounding the doorbell while Maggie decides on final accessories. Given the speed in which she makes such decisions now, it's a good idea for she and her mother to start deciding such things now. That way they may be close to a decision by High School. Just 11 years away.

Published May, 2003.

Driver's ed: neck brace required

Raising teenagers these days presents one new issue after another. But nothing compares to the stress of seeing your teenager start driving.

Car accidents are the leading cause of death for teenagers. Fourteen-year-olds show their stupidity wasting time on the Internet. Sixteen-year-olds show theirs drag racing in western Shawnee. Local headlines are full of the "thrill-seeking" high school junior who took his sophomore girlfriend hill jumping and two hours later got a two-for-one deal at the funeral home. The only teenager impervious to this belongs to a cloistered Mennonite community. And right now I'm on the hunt for one.

While teenagers have always been fixated on fast cars, video games have taken this to a new level. My kids learned to drive at age 5 with racing games. Those games encourage them to run red lights, jump bridges, ditch the cops and get the high score. Hollywood knows all this. Kids flock to the racing movies, like "Gone in Sixty Seconds" or "The Fast and the Furious." The latest in this genre is "The

Fast and the Furious: Tokyo Drift." No plot, just races and crashes, but no one gets even a scratch.

So the Keenan household has a boy who turns 16 in 49 days, seven hours and 10 minutes. And we have issues. Huge issues. So I did what any responsible dad would do. I left town on a business trip. My wife kept her cool. She enrolled him in driver's education school.

Used to be, drivers ed was part of the high school curriculum. A wildly popular class because you got to leave the school premises driving a car. At age 15. Back then, the driver's ed teachers was the exclusive domain of the football and basketball coaches. The jock teachers had a modest academic curriculum—driver's ed, study hall, and shop class. Driver's ed gave them the opportunity to pick up cigarettes, get their mail, and check out the field conditions at the rival school before the big game. All at the expense of the Board of Education. But someone wised up and pulled the plug. Leaving most parents with the "private school" options.

So driving schools began to flourish. Someplace in Lawrence offers an "all day" school—drop little Johnny off at 8 a.m. and by 5 he is ready for Talladega. Our choice was Twin City Driver Education in Overland Park. None of these classes come cheap. It takes top dollar to recruit an adult willing to ride with your son. Someone pre-fitted with a neck brace.

So last month I took my son to class. Saturday morning, 8 a.m. The students were in two groups. The girls were ready to go. They had been up for a couple hours, applying the flat iron to the hair, studying the materials, anticipating the test drive. The boys just crawled out of the back seat. Their brains were still in suspend mode.

For the driving instruction, Twin City will pick up your son or daughter. Meaning the students must give directions. The girls bring a map. The boys bring a live brain cell, maybe two. They blink a couple times, stare into space and say something brilliant like "Uh, do you know where Olathe is? I live close to that Subway shop."

So this month if you see a car on State Line Road with a "Student Driver, Twin City" sign, take the first exit.

Published June 2005.

Car pool line: a slice of life without peer

The school car pool line is a modern-day institution for kids, who, like ours, do not take a bus to school. This universe is normally the domain of the soccer mom. But on Friday, Dec. 19, it was my turn to pick up—the first time this school year I would partake. And about 30 seconds after arriving to the school parking lot, I had all the makings for an article.

The first thing I realized is that the car pool line is really no line at all. A line is a single assembly of things front to back, like ants marching in formation. Such a characterization would insult the moms who spent hours mapping out this elaborate arrangement.

The car pool line at my kids' school is a highly complicated, highly organized, extremely efficient matrix of two alternating rows of SUVs. Cars that sit so high that from 119th and Mission Road they can see Pike's Peak, and with two separate parking lots—upper and lower—each with its own rules.

You would expect nothing else from the moms in charge. At our school, like most in Johnson County, the soccer moms have more education, training and common sense that all the husbands combined. And it shows.

As I watched this unfold, the thought occurred to me that if the dads were in charge, it would make a Chinese fire drill look organized. Something akin to how Arrowhead stadium empties after a Chiefs loss. Think pickup gridlock where dads holler at their kids to dart between speeding cars. Dads cutting in line or never showing up at all, leaving little Johnny on the school curb until Child Services picks him up.

The next thing that occurred to me was this: As the moms sat in their cars waiting, picking up the children was the least relevant thing on their radar screens. This gathering was like bunko meets Sonic on the showroom floor during the busiest time of the year. There was a cell phone usage of obscene proportions. Moms dialing their moms, their sisters, their friends, and even drivers sitting two cars ahead of them. Moms poring over the mail, reading magazines, Christmas cards, jumping from car to car, sharing gossip, stories, trading gifts, you name it.

The third obvious thing was that the students could care less about their ride home. This was one big happy hour for them. The sun was shining bright, and the weather was unseasonably warm. It was one big recess with all the grades together. Sisters, brothers, cousins and neighbors were all hanging out and decompressing. The older students were holding court, commanding the attentions of the younger students. All were recounting the countless events that took place that day.

As each car pulled in front of the school, on cue from the teachers, the kids would disappear in the cars. And the line would shrink by one more car.

I was near the end, of course. My car filled up in seconds with the Keenans and a couple stragglers my wife instructed me to include in the haul. Five boys and one girl. As they jumped in, filling every seat, there was the excitement that comes with the last day of school for three weeks, plus a midday dismissal. For these passengers, it was a top 10 day of the year. And for the next 10 minutes, they were my captive audience.

I immediately engaged the boys.

"What did you do today?"
"Nothing."
"Learn anything?"
"No."
"How were your tests?"
"Boring."
I turned to my daughter, and before I could even ask a question, she began describing the most wonderful day with the most wonderful teacher, in the most wonderful school in the world, in colorful and entertaining detail.

The boys heard not a word of it. Their vacation had started about five hours earlier.

Published December, 2004.

Old-fashioned shoes right for my children

In today's society, "back to school" means a lot more than simply beginning classes all over again. It's a shopping extravaganza that some say is second only to Christmas in terms of spending.

And while shopping lists vary from one household to the next, they have at least one thing in common: new shoes. Little Johnny and Suzie always get new shoes for school. Guaranteed.

To be clear, I've got no problem with buying shoes, as a general proposition. Kids' feet grow to obscene proportions these days, giving their parents little choice. It's shopping that I detest.

Most shoe stores really aren't stores at all. They are sports bars with bad merchandise where the average employee just turned 13. They showcase most of their inventory on a huge wall—except for the size you need. That requires a salesman to disappear like he is visiting the Wizard of Oz to locate your son's size, which has changed in the preceding 90 days. And after the salesman is transported to another planet and then back again, he informs you they just sold their last 12D's. Been there.

And for all this aggravation you spend a small fortune. Kids shoes are priced out of sight, and I'm sick of it. For about $150, your son can wear the same shoes as a temperamental jock on the edge of the law. The "Allen Iverson" shoes were flying off the shelves at the same time the basketball star faced felony charges.

But it's more than simply cost. It's style too. The shoe display is like a Chinese wall of bad marketing mistakes. The shoe companies no doubt convened a focus group to help pick these styles. But where? Branson? The styles are more than ugly. They reflect the fashion sophistication of James Traficant's hair stylist. Today, they sell shoes with zippers.

Athletic shoes with zippers? Just imagine the announcer saying, "Play is stopped while Billy adjusts his zipper."

Only one time in my life have I seen a man wear shoes with zippers. In 1967, my uncle Pat traveled to the fashion capital of the world, Wichita, and returned with boots with zippers. We laughed at him. He claimed Johnny Carson wore them. We laughed louder. Two weeks later, he had a garage sale. Zipper boots were on special.

Shoes now feature springs on the heels. Maybe it's me, but putting my sons in shoes that help them bounce around the classroom sounds like an educational disaster of Titanic proportions. Other shoes have inflatable parts, which is another adolescent distraction ripe for science class. "Hey, let's blow up my new shoes! This is awesome!"

There are specialty shoes for something called "cross training." I have no idea what cross you train for with such shoes. They have shoes with retractable wheels. Brilliant! Observe your daughter repeatedly trip to the asphalt while you wait for her in the car-pool line!

My wife and I might not agree on much, but we are in complete harmony that our sons do just fine with old-fashioned shoes. Ones with strange things on them, such as shoe strings and rubber soles. In colors like blue and white. Made of canvas. Like Converse Chuck Taylor high-tops, for example. The finest shoes ever made.

Now, wearing shoes with Mr. Taylor's name won't guarantee the honor roll nor keep my sons out of the principal's office. But it's a start. A small one. And when my sons grow out of these babies by Christmas, it starts all over again.

What fun!

Published August 24, 2002.

Here are the rules for planning a disastrous birthday party

Over the last 15 years my wife has organized roughly 40 birthday parties with our four children.

Thirty-nine were huge disasters.

This is no criticism of my better half, mind you. Rather, it's an inevitable fact of all birthday parties. Parties for boys have the largest potential for Titanic-like outcomes, but girl parties have their own "issues."

Here is my recipe for birthday flops:

1. Raise your child's expectations. Tell your child early and often: "This is going to be the best birthday party ever. Better than the party with the hot-air balloon ride. Better than the party at the riding stable."

2. Invite the entire class and subdivision. A large turnout will demonstrate just how popular your child really is. Toss them all in the basement and watch time stand still.

3. Pick unusual venues to outdo everyone else. Skating parties can create fun memories when toddlers fall and chip their teeth. Petting zoos can be interesting, especially during goat-mating season.

4. Set aside several hours for the big event. Encourage parents to go shopping and be inaccessible. Accede to your son's demand that he can open all the presents first, not last. Dead time will encourage the brats to get creative.

5. Serve candy and sodas with loads of caffeine. It's a potent one-two combination kids love.

6. Coordinate with the Chief's schedule. Schedule the party during a Chief's game so dad can give his undivided attention. Let him drink a couple beers to "loosen him up" for when he needs to fill time with a couple makeshift magic tricks.

7. Invite scary clowns. Nothing can freak out toddlers quicker than a strange man with a bad wig, a red nose and shoes that curl up like those worn by the Wicked Witch of the West. Encourage the really shy ones to "go sit on his lap and get a special treat."

8. Get siblings involved. Brothers love it when their sister steals all the attention. Have ample water balloons, sling shots and BB guns around when they get bored.

9. Use those special candles that you can't blow out. Converting the cake into one big spitball will add to the special memories.

10. Leave the dog and the cake in the same room alone.

11. Forget about record keeping. Sort out later who brought which gifts.

12. Put a fitting end to the day by driving everyone home when it's over. Depend on the 9-year-old guests to help navigate the cul de sacs and dead ends found in most subdivisions.

This will extend the party another couple hours and improve your disposition considerably when you finally get home to pick up the mess.

Published March 19, 2005.

Cell phones and Teenagers

Everyone knows the story of the Alaska salmon. When young they live in the ocean, growing big and strong. When the time comes to start to family, they have to go upstream. This means swimming up rugged rivers, jumping up waterfalls, avoiding bears and something worse—fishermen from New Jersey. This is a fitting metaphor for parenting teenagers. The first half of our life is swimming downstream and living the good life. And then we get to raising teenagers.

And that's when the upstream part starts.

Parents constantly swim upstream. Sometimes the current is too great and you just give up. Take video games, for example. I'm sure that somewhere there is a family that defied the current of video games. Those homes where the teenagers spend their downtime reading "War and Peace" and practice for the spelling bee. Ever seen the movie "Spellbound"? That's not a Keenan home movie. At our place, the teenagers care more about their lineup for Madden 2007 than they do about spelling xylophone. So anyway, back to my story.

My wife and I find ourselves battling another current. This time it's the cell phone generation. This current has been swirling for sometime. It's pretty much everywhere these days. Take the back-to-school ads, for example, which include some cell phone deal. Since when did cell phones become part of the school routine? Who said Johnny needs pencils and a phone? What—to call someone during math?

Kids are getting phones at a younger age. I confirmed this at Overland Park Costco the other day when the "cell phone guy" was standing at the booth. No one getting within 100 feet of the man. Like he had the bird flu or something. So while my wife was inspecting a 500-pill supply of FiberCon, I asked him. "What's the youngest anyone has ever bought a phone? He paused and said, "Third grade."

He noticed my disgust. "But she got a great plan." I actually felt sick to my stomach. Some 9-year-old watching Barney and sending a text message.

All my kids' friends have a phone. Certainly every high school student has one. I lost that battle, but I'm happy to report that the two Keenans at Rockhurst have phones with one feature—to get calls from their mother just before their curfew. But it's middle school and grade school where I'm calling in reinforcements. But even there, many of their classmates have cell phones. And that includes my fifth-grade daughter. When I asked her to name names of cell phone users, 10 minutes later she was still in names starting with A.

A recent study in Britain says 51 percent of all 10-year-olds own a mobile phone, but that figure rises to 91 percent by the time children hit the age of 12.

Some of this is serious business. A recent survey of high school students that found that the top third of users—students who used their phones more than 90 times a day—frequently did so because they were unhappy or bored. Cell phones are an increasing distraction in school. Many schools ban them altogether, over the objection of—guess who—parents.

So back to the salmon. They eventually get upstream, lay eggs and die. I guess Mother Nature decided they had suffered enough. Raising teenage fish was too much to ask.

Published November 4, 2006.

Most dreaded words and other lists

Everyone has their lists. Comedians, authors, talk show hosts. I figured it's my turn.

•Three things you don't want to hear in your sons' parent-teacher conferences:

—"But there is some good news. He only hits during recess."
—"The principal has asked if he could join us for this meeting."
—"I think your son would do very well in a homeschool environment."

•People that I wish would go away and never return:

—Britney Spears
—Geraldo
—That red-headed guy who does those collect-call commercials
—Anyone who has ever been on "Survivor"

•Thinnest books

—"How to build a winning Pinewood Derby car" by Matt Keenan
—"Building a baseball dynasty on a shoestring budget" by George Steinbrenner

•Three things I wish they would bring back:

—Sister Mary Rose to teach and discipline my sons
—Cell phones the size of a brick so no one would dare to be seen with them
—Pay phones that cost a dime

•Movies I hope my children never see, no matter how old they get:

—"Animal House"
—"Something about Mary"
—"Rocky IX"

•Shocking surprises when you call customer service:

—"This call is not being recorded because no one would ever want to hear how poorly we treat you as a customer."
—"Your call is not important to us. That's why we put you on hold for two days."
—"Hello, this is Mary. I'm a real person. What can I help you with?"

•Things I would love to hear from the weatherman:

—"I don't care what the high temperature was on this date 50 years ago, and neither should you."
—"The weather is not going to change for the next week, so you can turn the channel now."
—"My forecast is probably wrong, but pay attention anyway."

•Statements never, ever uttered in the Keenan home:

—"Yes, I started the fight, and I'm sorry."
—"My poor grade has absolutely nothing to do with the teacher."
—"I got everything I wanted for Christmas."

•Sure things when I return from a long, stressful business trip:

—My car's gas gauge will be on empty.
—The ATM will tell me I'm overdrawn.
—My wife will park her car in the garage so it's the only one that will fit.

•Places my cell phone can't get a signal:

—Mission Road and Interstate 435
—Mission Road and 75th Street—Near Sprint's world headquarters in Overland Park

•Trends that I wish never got started:

—Tanning beds
—Jeans with waistlines previously reserved for refrigerator repairmen.

—Anything Britney Spears promotes.

Published March 16, 2002.

Girls and dances: Life gets complicated

These days raising high school kids has its share of challenges. Every parent knows that.

But one of things I'm still getting used to is how high school changes the social network. It just explodes.

On balance, it's all good. Teenagers make new friends, enjoy new experiences and all that.

But at our house, all of this is happening at the same time our son's communication skills have evaporated.

When the day arrived that our freshman son Tommy got invited to the Notre Dame De Sion dance is when things got very interesting very quickly.

Maybe our house if different, but simply learning that your son is invited to such things requires a congressional investigation.

After all, teenagers communicate differently these days. For example, no one under the age of 40 ever calls our home phone. In the old days the phone was the ultimate screening tool for parents. My older sister had boys calling the house all the time. Mom took all those calls.

"May I ask who is calling and what this is about?" "I'm sorry, I'm not sure we have ever met." "Has my daughter ever been in your car?" "Does the seat recline?" Are you Catholic?" "What's the name of the Pope?" "And his age?"

After a dozen other questions, mom would inform the big loser: "Thanks for the information. But Kathy just left. What message would you like to leave with me?"

Today these calls go directly to the teenagers' cell phones (during peak calling hours, of course). So parents don't have a clue on the social front.

Once a teen boy drops a dance-invitation bombshell, moms go into high gear. There is a mountain of information they need to know, now.

But gathering information from teen boys is, well, impossible.

My wife was undeterred. She turned off the Xbox and turned on a bright lamp.

"What color is her dress?" "Does she have a favorite floral shop?" "Do you have a tie that will match?" "Where is dinner?" "How are you getting there?" And on and on. After about three questions, my son faded into what appeared to be a medically induced coma. I never got to ask my questions, like "What's her name?" and a couple others that concern only dads.

But the information flow changed pretty dramatically.

We learned there would be a "photo shoot" at one of the parents' homes. This turned out to be an information bonanza. There were 10 couples present, with parents.

The contrasts were stark. Girls were primped and primed. They had spent the preceding 24 hours getting the hair, nails, toes, eyes, teeth and tan done. They were, as they say, quite "mature" and "together."

The boys, on the other hand, crawled out of bed just hours before. Some had bad hair. Others had horrific hair. Collectively, they looked like a clinical trial for Clearasil. It was Lady Diana meets Napoleon Dynamite.

The girls were making introductions, showing a high level of organization and planning. No detail was overlooked. This was their party and they were in charge.

The boys stood in a corner, staring at a corsage, wondering what it was and what you did with it.

Once the introductions stopped, the cameras started. Everyone had at least one, maybe two cameras. It was a massive solar flare.

There were various poses, groups, formations. It went on for like 10 minutes. I'm still seeing spots from the flashes.

When it was finally over one of the parents commented: "I'm almost out of film. Let's get a picture of the boys." "Can someone find them?"

Published January 21, 2006

4-step plan for waking teenagers

I'm not a doctor, but I play one at home. I'm a sleep specialist. And for most of the summer I've been conducting a clinical trial of sleep disorders. My patients: two of my teenager sons. The ones not yet old enough for a summer job.

On a typical summer day, they sleep until noon. When they get up, they eat five bowls of Lucky Charms and then move to the couch to partake in a yawning convention. Around dinner they eat a frozen pizza or, if they are lucky, get a brother to make a run to Taco Bell, and the cycle begins anew.

Amazingly, there was once a time when these slackers were infants, and they never slept. About age 2 they slept through the night and woke up at 5 in the morning and starting barking out commands from their crib. Things have changed, obviously.

I Googled this issue and found the Web chock full of chatter on this. Researchers point out that in teenagers, sleep-promoting hormone levels rise at different levels than in adults and infants. Basically this hormone—called melatonin—is one explanation for these bizarre sleep patterns. Their studies describe body clocks and things called "natural rhythms." They advocate later start times for schools, and some administrators have obliged. So the message is clear: Slackers can't help themselves.

I'm not buying any of this. I've learned that waking teenagers up requires a four-step plan.

1. The first wake-up call. Goal: Confirm life. Take a pulse. Never mind opening the eyes. That's hopeless. Is there breathing? Check for involuntary movements, skin tone, bowel sounds. This is no easy task. Little Johnny is buried under nine pillows, iPod headphones, two blankets and the stuffed teddy bear he's slept with since first grade. At that moment Johnny is enjoying his dream of all dreams—which means dreaming of sleeping. This is REM sleep so intense no doctor has yet to discover it. Think ol' Rip Van Winkle OD'd on Ambien. Rock their world with the announcement: "You have school today. Get up." You are attempting to drill down their brain and right now you are at the outer crust. Return in five minutes.

2. Visit No 2. Goal: Open the eyes. Get to the brain's outer core. Testing the hearing is a good start. You have already mentioned school and got no reaction. Take the next step. Tell them something outrageous. "The Royals swept the Twins." "Trent Green retired and has taken up with Willie Roaf." "Roy Williams is returning." "KU football coach Mark Mangino is at our front door wearing a Speedo." Do not leave until you see the whites of their eyes.

3. Visit No 3. Goal: Get them on their feet. Yank the blankets and pillows off the bed. Cold temperatures, next to cold water, are your best shot at this point. Now you must get to the inner core of their brain. Raise the voice, but since they tune out adults, talk like a teenager. "Dude, things are all messed up. We are running out of hot water." Or try this "Dude, your cell is broken. It's the cat. It's terrible." Shake their arms, their legs, their iPods. Once they stand up, leave the room but don't go far. You must prepare for the next visit.

4. Visit No. 4. Every teenager on the planet will attempt to crawl back to bed. So get back there quickly and sprinkle water on them. Resort to Oldies 95 if necessary. Blare it. Then dial their cell phone number. The distinctive ring will mean another social mixer at Town Center mall. And then wait for the announcement that will shake them to their core: "We are almost out of Lucky Charms."

Have the clothes laid out, the toothbrush ready, the backpack packed and the energy drink opened. They are walking but still not awake. Do something crazy—make them talk. Ask questions that require something other than, "I don't know." This part of the equation I have yet to master. When I figure that out, I'm going to learn whether my sons have any "natural rhythms." Stay tuned.

Published August 19, 2006

A Girl's diary and three brothers spell trouble

Daughters are special. Seven-year-old daughters are really special. But a daughter with three older brothers is divinely sent. About eight years ago, late one night, my wife told me that while she loved her three sons very much, she longed for a daughter. God willing, a miracle happened. Maggie Lee Keenan arrived. And as she grew up, she learned that her older brothers were both her best friends and her worst enemies.

Of late, it seems, her brothers have become more skilled at the second half of this equation. And as a consequence, Maggie has become a testament to Charles Darwin. She is one tough survivor. But there are certain battles she cannot win. Challenges that are so great, so insurmountable that even she cannot overcome them.

One of those battles concerns my daughter's penchant to commit highly personal thoughts to paper. Most of these find their way into a book, something called a diary. For most of my life, that word had been associated only with famous literary works. Until now.

To be sure, a young girl's diary is a wonderful thing. In our home, it's like the scent of fresh flowers in a musty men's locker room. Parents of second-grade girls know that their imaginations are boundless. Every day, a new wonderful journey. Maggie's diary is poetry for the soul, complemented with drawings of rainbows, butterflies and flowers more beautiful than Mother Nature herself could replicate.

But bringing a diary into our home is like leaving an Iraqi museum unguarded in the waning days of the Hussein regime. My sons can sniff out this treasure no matter how well it's been hidden. And like the archaeological treasures of Iraq, sooner or later, the diary will fall into the wrong hands. And though the price my sons pay for such transgressions should make them sheepish, they seem to think it's worth it to learn the inner secrets of their kid sister.

But, you say, don't diaries have a lock and key. To call it a "lock" would be like calling the Yugo a "car." This lock only raises the stakes for these boys. And once cracked, the secrets are fodder for the hellions. Boys don't think like girls. Strike that. Boys don't think at all.

They have zero appreciation for the fact that a second-grader can wish for things that do not involve guns, knives or explosives. Maggie's writings are the stuff of fairly tales. Walt Disney himself could not envision a more elaborate story. Castles, stagecoaches and weddings. And that's the first paragraph. Later writings include spending the rest of her life a billion miles from three brothers named Connor, Tommy and Robert.

But Maggie has survived in this jungle we call home because she is no fool. She knows that such a treasure trove of deep thoughts will, sooner or later, be read by the infidels who reside down the hallway.

So, invariably she includes nuggets about her brothers, tidbits that will send them into orbit. Observations about their female classmates and probable marriage partners. Intelligence a sister can gain only from hanging out and watching them interact with girls on the school playground. Her diary includes these verbal bombs that serve to drive the hyperactive tykes into a blustering babble.

This drill runs full circle about every other month. And then my wife heads out to purchase a new diary, with a new—stronger—lock, that permits my budding writer daughter to start anew. With a new prince, a new castle and new names for all her flock.

My wife was right: A daughter changes everything.

Boys have their own special qualities. But on days when my three sons are up to their latest tricks, I have a hard time thinking of any.

Published October 2003

Dad's Nightmare: Owning a Horse.

From time to time I lay in bed and wonder how my life got so complicated—three cars, four cell phones, and four children at three different schools. On weekends my kids like to invite over their friends, who seem to never leave.

Our home has seen sleepovers that run for two, maybe three nights. We need nametags for breakfast. Think "Family Circus" on steroids. I have other issues. My sons' homework problems become my problems. Some mornings I stare at my hair line and my expanding profile and dream of the days before children, when life was simple—really cheap.

And then my path crosses with another parent who puts my life into perspective, some poor soul who reminds me just how much worse my life could be.

I was attending my son's baseball game at 3 & 2 Stadium in Lenexa. And as we endured the ninth walk I started chatting with one of the other parents. This parent had older children. He had that "been there, done that" look to him. You know the type—thinning gray hair, large bags under the eyes, constantly checking his watch. I'll call him Frank. As he heard me describe my complicated life to another parent, he looked at me and smiled. "Young man, you have no problems. You don't own a horse."

I strained my ears. "I'm sorry. What did you say?"

He spoke louder this time: "I said own a horse. If you have a daughter, thank your lucky stars she does not have her own horse."

I closed my eyes to contemplate the enormity of what he just said. Two words I have never heard together in the same sentence, "own" and "horse."

When I opened my eyes, he had moved very close to me on the bleachers. "Do you have a daughter?" he asked. I nodded. And for the next three innings he had a very captive audience of one. I heard tales that would bring most sensible dads to their knees. And the story went something like this:

"You see, it starts out very innocently. Girls love horses. I can't understand it. But they do. They draw pictures of horses, they read books about horses, watch movies of horses. It's something in their genes. And moms know this. They wanted a horse when they were young. But they never got one. Because their dads had something few parents have these days—common sense. So it's one of those things that prompts your wife to say 'you wouldn't understand, you are a man.' And statements like these, for husbands, are not negotiable. We learn to just turn and find something else to occupy our time, like the cable remote." I nod.

"And one day you come home from work and something seems different. Your daughter has a bounce in her step. Your wife seems really nice to you. Something is up and you are about to find out what."

"Shortly thereafter, you find yourself a passenger in a car on a country drive. The car stops at a farm. But not a farm that raises corn or wheat. This farm raises animals. But I'm not talking about cows. I mean horses. The next thing you know, you are standing before a stable. In it is a beautiful horse, with a name like 'Gentry' or something like that. Your daughter climbs on the horse and rides in a circle. She smiles broadly. She looks absolutely beautiful. Mature. With me so far?" I nod. "Good, because now it gets interesting.

"Let me stop for a minute. This kind of thing tends to happen to those dads who have only one daughter. Let me guess—you have just one." I nod. Frank smiles broadly.

I wiped the sweat from my brow. "Wow," I say. "I guess it could be worse."

"It is," Frank says. "You see, a horse is one pet that you pay people to keep. You visit the thing on weekends. And when you do, you bring your wallet, because you have to pay them while you are there. To bathe the horse. Ride it. Feed it. Horses need their own veterinarian too. The vet has an assistant whose primary job is to send you a bill every 30 days. There is a trailer and a pickup to pull it. And let me tell you about the horse shows."

I interrupted him. "No more, please, unless the ending involves a horse burial." "Actually, I'm winding down. Just another hour." I cut him off again. "Stop please. My doctor warned me to monitor my blood pressure. It's peaking."

For the first time I noticed the scoreboard. The game was over. The score did not matter to me. Getting home immediately did.

Published May 20, 2006.

Dance Recitals: I have major issues!

Girls take dance lessons. Whether it's ballet, dance or just letting them move around to bad music, young girls eventually will end up in a recital before brothers, sisters, parents, grandparents, uncles, aunts. It's a rite of passage everywhere.

Last year, this cultural phenomenon arrived at our doorstep. But when my wife enrolled my daughter in dance, I hardly noticed. That changed a couple of months later. It got my attention when money began departing from my wallet on a regular basis. Going broke for your daughter—your only daughter—I'm somewhat used to. But watching those dollars go toward recital outfits more appropriate for someone who does stage work at Caesars Palace, I have a problem with. Maggie was 6, not 16. So the notion of her wearing slinky outfits with boas, glitter and makeup bothered me. A lot.

So I see all this develop, and, like any good husband, I shut up. I know that when it comes to issues about my daughter, there are two battles. Those you fight and lose. And those you don't even bother fighting. But this recital thing was unchartered waters for both my wife and I, and so we collectively absorbed it slowly. But it was coming quickly. And at some point, my wife informed me that this recital was not solely the domain of my daughter. That this recital featured a "father/daughter" dance. A dance that required the fathers to wear specially selected shirts and shorts to join their daughters onstage.

This made no sense to me. Recitals are to showcase the girls. Alone. Sticking a clumsy 43-year-old dad onstage alongside such innocence invites a disaster of unthinkable proportions. It's like launching the Exxon Valdez over Niagara Falls. "You better plan on making the rehearsals," she said. "You can embarrass yourself. But you can't embarrass Maggie." Message delivered.

So almost overnight my daughter's recital became my recital. Which meant Friday night rehearsals, my own outfit (purchased exclusively from just one place), and squeezing a three-night recital into an already clogged spring calendar. Weeks before the show, I was spending Friday nights in a strip mall, near a Radio Shack and video arcade. They generously called it a "studio." There I got to hang out with other dads who, like me, failed to read the fine print on the dance class brochure.

At the rehearsals we stood in front of wall-sized mirrors as our dance instructor—wrapped in spandex—barked out commands like a five-star general. It was Patton meets the "Attack of the Clones." This was no Kodak moment, trust me.

All of this culminated in three nights last May. And once concluded, my monthly credit card bill included the cost of 10 tickets, refreshments, studio shots of Maggie, an exclusive videotape, programs, outfits and the tuition, of course. Room additions come cheaper.

So this year, my wife helped Maggie find a new dance instructor. With new outfits. It's called "Musical Theater." Where precious first-graders have the stage all to themselves. My kind of recital.

Published May 17, 2003

Moms who worry and husbands who don't

Moms tend to worry a lot.
Some moms, like a few I know well, worry about most everything these days. Moms begin to fret right about the time their children get old enough to leave their plastic bubble and explore a world outside the front door.

This is no criticism of my wife or any mom, to be sure. We live in an age defined by an entirely new vocabulary of stressors—Amber alerts, Megan's law, sleeper cells, dirty bombs, WMD, tsunamis, West Nile, antibiotic resistant germs, just to name a few. So when little Johnny heads out the door, moms get nervous.

When this happens in our home, my wife shows her fondness for the c-word.

"Mom, I'm going to a movie."
"OK, Tommy. Be careful!"
"Mom, it's a movie, not Iraq!"
"I don't care. Be careful!"

Another instance:
"Mom, I'm riding my bike up the street."
"Wear your helmet! And be really careful!"
Sporting events, especially baseball games:

"Mom, my ride is here for my baseball game."
"Wear your protective cup! And your mouth guard. And your helmet. And be careful!"

These admonitions typically bounce off my kids' ears. But moms know this, of course. They are moms. They know everything. So they do more. They plan ahead and follow up. They use their cell phones prodigiously, interrogate the child upon his arrival home and leave nothing to chance.

Last year, my wife packed three trunks for Boy Scout camp. Her "safety plan" included enough mosquito repellent to drown every bug in St. Clare county, a lifetime of sunscreen and a 10-pack of toilet seat covers. The boys used none of them.

Moms hope to never rely on their husbands to execute the "safety plan." My wife says I'm easily distracted by anything and everything all the time.

For example, when the kids are at the park, and she tells me to "watch the children," no self-respecting man would take that literally. You can read the paper, make phone calls or even nod off and still be "watching" the little tykes.

And nothing can juice up a moms' stress more than a vacation. You are leaving their comfort zone and mixing with strangers—often driving or flying great distances, which means a loss of control, anxiety, panic.

Throw in bad weather, cold temperatures, and a 9-year-old daughter on snow skis, and it's medication time. So when the Keenans headed to Keystone, Colo., for spring break, and my wife decided to take a break from the mountain, the custody of her only daughter was in my capable hands. I got a lecture with all the buzz words.

"It's cold out. It's snowing. Do not let Maggie separate for a second. Blah, blah."
I reassured her: "It's fine. It's OK. Chill."
But my wife had a plan, which I discovered at the end of the day after I delivered the angel child back to her mom's secure arms.

In Maggie's coat was a note, which my wife placed in her zipper pocket. The note read something like this:

"If you have found this note it's because my daughter has been separated from her dad. I asked my husband to ski with my daughter and never lose Maggie.
"HE FAILED IN THE ONE THING I ASKED OF HIM.
"Maggie Keenan is my only daughter. I will come pick her up. Do not bother trying to locate my husband. Here are four numbers where you can reach me.
"I am expecting your call.
"913-xxx-xxxx (cell phone)
"970-xxx-xxxx (condo number)
"913-xxx-xxxx (my sister's number)
"913-xxx-xxxx (my mom's number)

"If you should run across Maggie's dad, please inform him that there are some hotel vacancies in the Dillon area and he should get a room there. He will also need to find his own way back to Kansas City. And a good divorce lawyer.

"And while you have Maggie, please be careful."

Published April 16, 2005.

In need of a spring break trip? Try the back yard

This is spring break week. And according to my children, we are the only family on the planet that has not enjoyed the last seven days from a cruise ship or on a mountaintop. Like most things, they are misinformed. I know of at least two families in town. Yours and mine.

My children don't understand that spring break is a scam perpetrated by travel agents. It's not really spring, and my kids don't need a break. They just had one. A month-long Christmas vacation and then four snow days.

As I see it, the terms "family vacation" are a true oxymoron. We learned this the hard way. A couple years ago we flew to Disney World. In addition to going broke, I learned that airline toilets present unique challenges to my sons, who have difficulty hitting a target even in the absence of mid-air turbulence. Airport security has its own issues. My kids don't understand that "special screening" is not a term of distinction. So here we stay.

Things are just more complicated today than they were 30 years ago. Back then, everyone took vacations. Or that's what we called them. We piled in the station wagon and drove 90 mph to Colorado and then turned around and sped back home. Pikes Peak was the one thing we could focus on for more than a minute. Everything else was a blur.

Parents and children occupied separate worlds. And a car served as the perfect metaphor for this reality. There was an iron curtain between the front and back seats. Mom and Dad sat up front and "visited." Kids got tossed in the back and rolled around, fought and never touched a seat belt. With the wind howling and the temperatures in the 90s, Mom would order us to take a nap. The only other time we intersected was when Dad reached around the back seat to spank someone. He took corrective measures without taking his eyes off the road. Whoever he smacked deserved it. It was frontier justice. It worked.

We owned a 1972 Town and Country station wagon. Ninety-nine percent of the components were either solid steel or vinyl. Cruise ships come smaller. In mid-July the seats could fry bacon.

In the mid '70s we installed a CB radio for these trips. The antenna was something NASA invented and extended some 10 feet off the trunk. This kept us occupied. In the dead zones on Interstate 70 my kid brother would do meek impersonations of truckers and drop verbal bombs on various social topics like gun control. It was great fun.

Our trips had a couple of other sure things. For some reason, we never owned a cooler. Lunch was bologna sandwiches. The mayo baked and smelled like dead fish. We still ate it. We shared one bottle of Dr. Pepper for five kids. We swapped it, oldest to youngest, each one taking a long swig, with follow-up sips. By the time my younger sister got her turn, that bottle had more floaters than an aquarium full of sea monkeys. We did not stop for anything (and I mean anything) until Goodland and then Limon, Colo.

At some point during this odyssey, Colorado passed a law banning the picking of flowers. This became an obsession for Dad, who previously did not know Colorado even had flowers. For us, this made them prized possessions. At roadside stops we would stare at the vegetation while my dad would declare, "Pick one of those suckers, and you go to jail." Family horse rides were another given. Permitting a teenager the privilege of staring at the posterior of a horse and waiting for the action to start is more fun than Disney World.

So if your children are like mine—whining about their backyard vacation—remind them that school starts again in just two days. That should improve their disposition.

Published March 20, 2004

Role of pediatrician comes with a pedestal

Right before Christmas my fifth-grade son got sick with the flu. The only person more miserable than him was my wife. Moms have some genetic code where they feel the pain of their sick child. Dr. Phil probably knows this. Men have no such genetic flaw, of course. They can't afford to feel pain. They have to work to pay the pharmacy bills that pile up overnight. And the one person my wife trusts completely for support was not me. It was the family pediatrician—the world's smartest, kindest, most patient man.

We call our pediatrician Jeff Almighty. Whatever he says to my wife, on any subject, is gospel. If he told my wife at 9 a.m. to live the rest of her life in a cave in the Ozarks, she would be in Branson by noon. He's so good he can't take any more patients. It's the only exclusive club to which we belong.

But that's true of all pediatricians. They are always right. And always accessible. They keep weekend hours. They take phone calls in the middle of the night. Their clinics are warm and inviting. They don't have one of those bullet-plated windows that separates the staff from the patients. Their nurses are pleasant. When you call their office, you don't get a recording that lasts for five minutes that insults your intelligence by saying, "If this is a real emergency, hang up the phone and call 911."

Pediatricians also don't waste your time or money. They can diagnose an ear infection in seconds. They drive beat-up cars. Kids love 'em. Moms love 'em. Dads have to love 'em. Otherwise they come to love a new word: ALIMONY.

These docs pass out more drug samples than drug reps. They get more Christmas cards than school principals. Pediatricians receive the privilege to declare to proud parents that their sons are in the 95th percentile in height, their daughters are in the 45th percentile in weight, and both favor their mother in every important respect. Husbands, for all intents and purposes, are mere donors. Fathers also entrust pediatricians to perform a delicate surgery on their newborn sons, a procedure with zero margin of error.

One of the most beloved pediatricians, Dr. Benjamin Spock, was one of the best-selling authors of all time. His book, Baby and Child Care, sold more than 50 million copies. He was adored the world over. Yet when he advocated unpopular positions on social issues, like the Vietnam War, moms everywhere did not flinch. They still loved him. When he died, it was an outpouring reserved for presidents and heads of state.

Marcus Welby was no pediatrician, but he acted like one. Howard Dean is a doctor but clearly not a pediatrician. If he were, he would be curing sick kids instead of begging for votes in places like Dubuque and Des Moines.

Dads stand absolutely no chance against pediatricians. When the son has a sore throat on the day of his football game, the dad always concludes: "He's fine. Give him some Tylenol and let the little guy go hit someone." The mom immediately disagrees, feels his forehead and concludes: "He's got strep throat. I'm sure of it." And two hours later, the pediatrician confirms her suspicions: "Yep, it's strep. Playing in the game is a horrible idea. No one could possibly suggest otherwise." Game over.

So just as Dr. Jeff predicted, on day seven my son got back his temperature, color, strength, energy and smile. And so did his mother. And life returned to some degree of what in our home is normal. And once again our family pediatrician's standing as a first cousin to God himself remained secure.

Published January 17, 2004.

Piano to electric guitar: a painful journey

Music, the experts say, makes for smarter kids. Parents hear this and promptly enroll their sons and daughters in music lessons. In our home, we chose piano. But this was no family vote.

You see, as all parents know, kids (more particularly, boys) hate piano. They detest it. Boys hate anything involving finger movement that does not involve pulling triggers, firing rubber bands or, depending on their age, picking their noses.

They never practice and consequently detest lessons. Reminding them of piano lessons—especially while they are in the middle of a game on their PlayStation 2—prompts horrific reactions: the drop-to-the-ground, neck-goes-stiff, eyes-roll-in-the-back-of-the-head, call-the-parish-priest right now reaction—the kind of drama only seen on the History Channel.

Over the years I have tried to motivate my sons to practice, pointing out famous piano players—Harry Connick Jr., Ray Charles, Paul McCartney.
They bring up their own list—mainly Liberace.

Piano teachers do their share to motivate. They tend to be patient, kind, soft-spoken and great liars. Over the years they have told me, without flinching, "Your son did well today. I see improvement!"

These are laugh-out-loud fabrications, of course. Admitting the obvious means one fewer student and one step closer to a second career selling seamless siding.
I don't care much for piano recitals. If I had a house full of girls, that would be one thing, but I don't.

Girls make these red-letter, five-star events, with a new dress and huge bow to show to the grandparents and cousins who show up and hog the front couple rows of seats.

For the boys (at least our boys) these things inevitably conflict with a ballgame, or if not, seem to fall smack dab in the middle of the NCAA basketball tournament.

Our kids get upstaged by those who can play something other than chopsticks. These are the shrimpy kids who divide their time practicing for either piano or the upcoming spelling bee.
So all of this came full circle in the last year.

My oldest son found payback for those hours spent in the basement of the Prairie Village Toon Shop. He ditched the piano and picked up the guitar.

He taught himself, which saved us a small fortune. But the acoustic became the electric, later paired with a huge amplifier, and a then a microphone. Next came a band formed with a couple Rockhurst classmates, and suddenly this music thing was disturbing my normal sleep patterns. They cut a CD and made a hundred copies, which Connor's brothers learned are terrific Frisbees.
So now I lie in bed at night and imagine groupies, slacker conventions and a lifestyle hardly consistent with high academic achievement—which was the original goal, of course.

It could be worse, I remind myself. For starters, they have "band practice" at the drummer's home a couple miles away, conveniently. His parents are either deaf or will be shortly. No band would be complete without a name, and this band has had six. Presently it's called "West Emma."

And then, out of the blue, West Emma debuted in a "Battle of the Bands" competition at Blue Valley North High School just last month.

My wife attended and reported that she was the only female there whose belly button was not exposed. She also stood out because her skin color was olive, not spray-on bronze. Some eight bands "played," girls screamed, and now I'm sleeping even less.

I have no idea where this will end. But now my third son—who attended the battle and was apparently mesmerized by it all—now wants his own guitar.

I sure hope he won't disturb me while I hide in my bedroom curled in the fetal position.

Published March 2004

Dad's arguments come full circle when discussing class ring

High School students have a tough life. They have to struggle with all kinds of serious issues. Like recharging their Ipods, getting a full cell phone signal, sleeping in 'til noon on Saturday. Other issues don't seem to bother them in the least. Like driving on an empty tank, finding a summer job, having money in their wallet. So in the category of "judgment," we've got issues. Imagine, then, my interest level when I heard that my high school junior was contemplating ordering his high school class ring.

Like most things, I learned that this was under discussion very late in the game. Mother and son had vetted this topic extensively. But no one asked for my opinion, which meant I needed to express it. So recently one evening over dinner I was able to hold court on this topic. And I began by explaining to the assembled audience that long ago my dad was dumb. At times, it seemed, he was a complete idiot. At some point in college, I realized he wasn't stupid, just misinformed. Then I went to law school. There I came to accept that he was pretty smart. And at some point more recently, when the stress of my parenting job exceeded the stress of my legal job, I began to appreciate just how brilliant my dad really is.

By now I was parading around our kitchen. My lecture was in high gear. My dad was smart, in part, because he used a word that the Leawood Keenan kids don't hear enough. It's a simple word but carries a powerful punch: "No."

I went on. I explained that in 1977 I was about to order my class ring from Jostens, the same company about to receive my son's order. They were a small company, but growing fast. Back then there were two or three expensive options when it came to class rings. All my friends were getting the white gold or yellow gold options, with a red or black stone, representing our school colors. That's when my dad used his favorite two-letter word.

From the perspective of a 16-year-old, my dad needed to be educated. So that's what I did. I explained that this was more than just a ring, it was a statement of town pride. Especially in places like Great Bend, which only had one high school. The salesman told us that, and it was so true! But it was so much more than that, of course. There was class pride at stake. And the class of 1977 was special. It was remarkable because it included me and my friends. Dad listened carefully, nodded, and repeated his magic word.

I suspected this would be an uphill battle. On most parenting issues my parents' position was largely shaped from mistakes learned with my oldest sister, Kate. Her ring order was not constrained by any sensible budget. She was then, as they say today, "big in the bling." There were other things big about my sister—namely hair, dreams and boyfriends. She also had a sizeable ring collection, thanks to the aforementioned men in her life. Most of her teenage years she was "going steady" with one guy or another.

So anyway, when it came to me, it was payback time. But my dad wasn't draconian. He let me place an order. But let's just say that ring was of the quality you could buy with a quarter in the King Louie lobby. It was composed of some metallic alloy that turned my finger a shade of blue-green. It was prone to scratches and discoloration. I wore it for about a month. And then it disappeared forever.

So as my Leawood listening audience was about to pull the plug, I started to transition into some other life's lesson. My wife interrupted me. "Stop. Sit down. Your son doesn't want an expensive ring. He is OK with something modest. It's under control. Plus we have heard this story before."

Class adjourned.

Published April 1, 2006

Childhood sandpit still has magic.

Today is March 3, which means spring is around the corner. So to put us in the right mood, this column is about summer. You see, this is a fish story, but unlike some, this one is not prone to embellishment. Not one bit. And it goes like this.

The home where I was raised in Great Bend, Kan., is still in the family. One reason why it's special is that it's on a lake. It's actually a pond, and the locals would say it's a sand pit. But it has been around since the Stone Age, and growing up there 40 years ago, we fished in that thing every day. And over the years we caught huge fish there. In 1972 my older brother Tim caught a state-record fish there, a 36-pound fish called a buffalo head. We also caught catfish, flatheads, largemouth bass, you name it. We had countless broken fishing lines, witnessed stray dogs disappearing from the water surface and observed huge splashes at dusk and dawn.

So my sons have heard these stories and seen the photos, but have shown only passing interest. So fast forward to last July Fourth. As we always do, we loaded up the Suburban and headed west. My three sons brought the usual collection of non-Keenan tag-alongs, two eighth graders named David and Christian. Part of the negotiated agreement was that we would fish the pond hard, which included setting trotlines—long lines with a billion hooks. For two days we battled snapping turtles, bullhead and perch, but caught nothing significant. We checked the line on July 3 and came up empty. And as we dropped the line to the lake bottom I felt the magic of the sand pit was gone.

Later that day we drove past the point where the line extends deep in the water. The road sits above the water surface, maybe 15 feet, so you can look down directly into the pond. My youngest son said, "Let's check the line." Near the lake's surface, directly over our line, was a large shadow that was stationary. It was the shape of a fish, something resembling a Great White. My uncle Bob—who also lives on the lake—happened to walk by at that moment. Uncle Bob is 84 and has caught fish all over the world. His stories would make the late Harold Ensley sheepish. Bob also has a penchant for speaking precisely. He stared at the shadow, narrowed his brow, and said, "That fish weighs 50 pounds." But what he said next still gives me chills: "And it's on your line."

What followed was a blur. There was a mad dash to the paddle boat, which was resting on the shore. This paddle boat is to watercraft what the Yugo was to automobiles. It leaks horribly and for 362 days of the year it sits empty and gathers rust. And then comes the Johnson County invasion. And in that moment, caution wasn't just tossed to the wind. It was drop-kicked into the next county. The boat was designed for two passengers. At 2:36 p.m. on July 3, it had six.
There was no time for a lifejackets. No mothers were there to scream, "Stop!"

We paddled to where the line was attached to the bank. One of our Johnson County guests grabbed the line and began to pull it. There was immediate "pull back"—like tug-of-war with something seriously PO'd. And as we paddled over the hot spot, there was a swirling of water, yelling and cussing—yes, cussing. Every bad word had the word "holy" as a prefix. It was OK. God understood. We were about to come face to face with Satan himself.

Uncle Bob was standing above us on the bank, barking out commands: "Don't horse it! Don't horse it!" And as the beast rose to the surface, the shouting stopped. Breathing was enough of a challenge. It was, without question, the largest freshwater fish in North America. It was not 4 feet. It was closer to 5. A carp. Its girth was beyond estimation. Bigger than anything at Cabela's or Bass Pro. By now the boat was tipping at a 45-degree angle, water was pouring in and our guardian angels were earning combat pay. The fish was swirling water, and as my 15-year-old son extended the net, I knew this endeavor was hopeless. It was like shoehorning a whale into a grocery sack.

Just when the net brushed its head, it was gone. And for about two seconds, no one said a word. It was like we let Bigfoot, Sasquatch and the Loch Ness monster escape. Leaving in its place one great fish story.

Looking back, for those six or seven minutes, five Johnson County teenagers and one 47-year-old were transported back to the glory days of 1972. To a time when three Keenan boys spent every summer day on that pond, with a fishing pole and tackle box, looking for the next state record.

That event, however brief, is something no Hollywood producer could ever script. And the next day, as we pulled away from the Keenan homestead, my 14-year-old son looked at me and said: "When we come back, we are going to get that fish."

Published March 3, 2007

2

Schools

In 2007, we have children in high school, middle school, and grade school. We also have four cars, five cells phones and an industrial sized container of Tylenol for all the headaches.

Dress code makes tuition money well spent

My son is attending high school this year. He will be a freshman at Rockhurst. Its academic reputation is above reproach, of course, and I've heard something about its sports teams.

But as a lifelong Kansan, the notion of my kids attending school in Missouri is a bit discomforting, and the tuition price tag doesn't make me feel much better. The last time I checked, the public schools in Johnson County were pretty darn good and did not come with a separate invoice. So this was no quick or easy decision.

But once the decision was made, he applied, was accepted and enrolled.
And about three weeks ago, a thick packet arrived with all kinds of information for the parents and student. Buried in the bottom was the dress code. All of a sudden, the tuition became a bit more palatable. The author of this concise document should be in charge of the IRS. There is more information, in clear unambiguous terms, on this one-page document than in the entire tax code. It arrived on the back side of the letter from the dean of students welcoming my son to the class. Some of this is worth sharing.

Take hair, for example. "Hair must be clean, and well groomed.... Extremes in hairstyles (lines or designs, uneven patches of hair, ponytails, unnatural color, etc.) are not allowed. Tails are forbidden."

So far, so good. Keeping my son's hair brown and not purple is very important to his mother.
Shoes: "Only dress shoes or loafers may be worn, and they must be worn with full-length socks."
"Socks must extend above the ankles. Half-socks (anklets) are not permitted."
My sons call these "cool." I call them history.

Jewelry: "Earrings, studs, or devices meant to hold open a pierced ear or body part" gone.
Hats: "Hats or caps may not be worn inside the building at any time."
The words "at any time" bounced around in my head. "How refreshing," I said to myself.
Shirts: "Hawaiian and/or loud prints, flannel shirts" banned.

And how do you wear them?
"Shirts must be tucked in at all times, before, during and after school."
"Work clothes, baggy pants, cargo pants, bell bottoms, denims, jeans, worn or faded pants are not allowed."
"Jackets or hooded sweatshirts must not be worn around the building and must be kept in a student's locker."
And it concluded with the reminder that the dean of students has godlike powers to ban any other creative mix or match.

That pretty much sums it up. Bad clothes sometimes defy description; it's like Supreme Court Justice Potter Stewart's opinion about pornography: He couldn't describe it, but he knew it when he saw it. And any school administrator who cannot only define a dress code—but also anticipate the ways creative teenagers will attempt to circumvent it—is someone worthy of teaching my son.
So I'm excited about this new school. My son is, too—despite the fact his back-to-school shopping won't include a trip to Abercrombie & Fitch or Tommy Bahama.

Published August, 2003

Graduation celebration: Please count me out

May means graduation. Used to be, graduation ceremonies were reserved for young adults who actually accomplished something. That reality died in the

'80s—roughly when someone came up with the idea of participation trophies. So now graduation ceremonies extend to the middle schools and sometimes to the preschools.

And because my son is finishing eighth grade, I am the not-so-proud father of a graduate.

But I got issues with all this.

Call me strange, but I got a problem with honoring 13-year-olds whose only noteworthy accomplishment is their proficiency in applying Clearasil after gym class, kids whose claim to fame is having a brain they never use, kids who finish eighth grade because state law says they have no choice.

As best I can tell, there are five sure things about middle school graduations:

1. Money. Teenagers spend money faster than Paris Hilton. Graduation gives them an excuse. Graduates need caps, gowns, graduation photos and invitations. They expect gifts like iPods and cell phones. They demand new clothes. And that includes boys, who no longer will wear whatever you grabbed on sale at Wal-Mart. Now they expect something from those American Eagle/Abercrombie-type stores that feature naked teenage models.

Girls have no clothes budget. They get what they want, and moms are happy to oblige. It is, after all, graduation.

2. Moms. See No. 1. All moms are teenagers by proxy. I would say more but May is also home to Mother's Day. "Be nice," my wife said.

3. Checking out. Middle-school kids think they are seniors. So they act like it. They stop caring about school work in early spring. Throw in warm temperatures, and they check out and never check back in. The social calendar replaces the homework calendar.

A typical discussion in our home:

Father: "Let me see your grade card."

Son: "Dude, school is over. I'm graduating, OK?"
"Son, it's February."

"Oh, my gosh, dad. Get a clue."

4. Tears and hugs. Teenage girls are drama queens. Graduation is a hormonal tsunami.

The moms at our school make what is known as the "eighth grade video"—a compilation of baby photos and other pictures for every student, matched with sentimental music. It's actually the highlight of the entire graduation, but it prompts a cry fest not seen since Roy Williams left KU. Kleenex starts flying everywhere.

Following that, the hugfest begins—girls hugging girls, moms hugging girls, moms hugging moms, dads staring at their watches, boys looking for the nearest exit.

For girls, the only life they know is over. They can't cope. They are leaving their best friends. It's horrible, really. Until they reunite the next day at the pool, and then the next day at the mall, and next day at the theater.

5. Parties. See 1-4. Moms plan parties. Mothers of graduating daughters plan "social events." Dads play no role, other than writing the checks. Some schools have pre-parties, post-parties and secret parties.

This begins the fully sanctioned "boy/girl" parties, leading the girls to showcase an onslaught of strapless, backless halters, falters, spaghetti straps, tube tops and anything else that dangles by a thin string. Hair and nails get a workout. Fake-bake tans come alive. Here, middle school is no different than high school because teenage girls not only act like seniors, but they also look like them, too.

These boy/girl parties are chaperoned with a battalion of nosy moms ready to sniff out the "bad kid" who has an agenda that doesn't include signing yearbooks. Moms are like biblical good shepherds—finding the lost sheep who aren't lost and don't want to be found. There is usually groping somewhere, someplace at every party.

I figure all this will end by mid-June. Someone wake me up when it's over.

Published May 14, 2005

My kids, homework and the back seat of my station wagon

In our home, the return of school brings with it fall sports and everything else that starts in September: Boy Scouts, music lessons and rain that never stops. School also forces my wife and me to re-establish limits on the usual summer excesses of television, video games and Internet messaging. This invites conflict, argument, resolution and then conflict all over again. All within minutes.

But the return of school, more than anything else, equates with the return of homework. Lots of it. It's not simply the volume, although that has grown dramatically. It's the instructional demands in nightly homework that has converted my wife and me to more than just supportive parents. We are unpaid tutors.

For the most part, this is a function of our children growing older, with more difficult subjects and greater academic challenges. I accept that. But at the same time, fifth grade is not college, and Nativity Parish school is not Pembroke.

So to switch from the dog days of summer to the helter-skelter existence of school—all within a two-week period—transforms our home into "Family Circus" on steroids. And it's the nightly studies that often get short shrift.

Over these years, I've learned there are three sure things when it comes to homework:

1. Last minute discoveries. No matter the planning, our children discover their most important assignment right before bedtime. That work then ends up being completed in the back seat of my car on the way to school. My kids can do more homework while I drive the four miles to school than any other students on the planet. This has converted my car into a mobile library, with pencils, pens, paper clips and paper easily available somewhere on the car floor; tutors (brothers); and a phone to call mom for more guidance. One son memorized the capitals of all 50 states in the course of 10 blocks. I figure that if we simply moved a couple of miles farther from school, my kids would be National Merit Scholars.

2. My homework is your homework. My wife and I are willing partners in the homework tasks. We serve as Tony Robbins-like coaches to our dispirited sons and daughter. But my children readily confuse the distinction between teacher and pupil. This is never more true than when it comes to the dreaded class projects. For the uninformed, typically these are massive undertakings that can consume an entire weekend. For example, the favorite in our school is the "Invention Convention." It's a clever and intriguing concept. On paper. But when the creation, design and construction of such ideas is left to third-graders, it's one more deadline on my work calendar with the heading: invent volcano.

3. You are an adult, you must know everything. Parents are supposed to know everything. What we don't know, we fake. Just ask my wife. But not even 11 combined years of college education is much help when it comes to sixth-grade grammar. Last year, I discovered that the easy part was hard; the hard part, impossible. Nouns, verbs and adverbs I can figure out. But verbs used as nouns, predicate adjectives, indirect objects and complete subjects involve brain cells that died sometime in the early '70s. And nothing I have done since college has revived any of that gray matter. So invariably when I "assist" my son with the homework projects, he returns with the graded paper the next day and declares in a loud voice for his siblings to hear, "Dad, you got a D. Way to go!"

So please don't call me anti-education when I confess that I'm less than excited about the return of school. Sure I giggle at the prospect of dropping them at school every morning, but their problem becomes my problem every evening. And while they know homework starts all over again, they also know that two middle-aged allies will stand in their corner, with a well-stocked Volvo station wagon waiting in the wings.

Published August 2002.

The conduct grade and the golden days of discipline

These days, schools have lots of rules to maintain order. They can take the form of warnings, reminders, infractions and, if necessary, early morning detentions. Dean Wormer in the movie "Animal House" was partial to the double secret probation.

Rockhurst High School has its own system. It's called JUGS, which is some Latin acronym that the students have converted to "Justice Under God." The Jesuits have this down. They know that the international language is not music. It's pain. And it works.

But this is no trash piece for discipline. Schools have to maintain order, but I long for the good ole days—the time when schools had a grade for "conduct" and the parents handled the punishment, which typically involved the international language.

Some schools wimped out and adopted the "Satisfactory/Unsatisfactory" approach. But the great schools gave students a letter grade—A through F.

It was clear. No questions. No comments. No further elaboration needed. One letter in the alphabet spoke for all the others.

I miss those days.

It saves me time during each parent-teacher conference when my first question is "How is my son's behavior?" and 10 minutes later I'm still taking notes, leaving no time for less important topics, like math and English.

Anyway, 30 years ago St. Patrick's Grade School in Great Bend had it all right.

We got a conduct grade.

Back then, girls got A's, boys, C's. Girls were angels; boys, devils. Not much has changed since then.

In the Keenan home with three boys and two girls, the disparity was never clearer. And all of this came to a head in the fall of 1968.

That was the year my kid brother Marty brought home is grade card. His conduct grade: D minus. It was really an "F," but Sister Monica cut him a break.

There was no academic confidentiality back then. Word spread of Marty's new low like a tumbleweed barreling across Barton County—right to the front door of 3616 17th Street.

It was a long time coming, of course.

That was the year Marty and his buddy Bobby Fiest discovered the tunnel under the school and spent half the quarter inspecting the heating and cooling pipes in the basement—not during recess, during math!

When Marty arrived home with the grade card, mom said what she always said: "Wait 'til your father gets home."

When dad did arrive, Marty did what any self-respecting seventh-grader would do: He locked himself in the bathroom.

When he emerged, he got spanked, grounded and endured punishment not seen since my older sister used the f-word.

The Geneva Convention had no jurisdiction over Larry Keenan.

Marty didn't help his cause much, blaming Sister Monica, and the principal—who also wore a habit, mind you. His blame game continued until he insulted our priest, the Pope and half the Holy See.

I watched from a safe distance and refused to throw him a lifeline. I had my C and no fear of retribution. This was his problem, his solution.

Many weeks later Marty raised his conduct grade and several weeks after that completed his prison sentence, which was served in his bedroom.

Those were the days.

Published February, 2005

The school nurse: Part teacher, part doctor, all powerful

It's the flu season, which means that students are busy infecting their classmates and half the neighborhood. And who does this reality elevate to a position of immense power? The soccer mom? Nope. The pediatrician? Negative. The most powerful person on the planet? The school nurse.

The school nurse has power over the soccer mom. She can yank moms from the Nordstrom parking lot to the grade school parking lot. She can empty out Starbucks/Einstein Bros./Hi Hat coffee shop with one call, that's all. "Mrs. Keenan, Robert has a headache, fever and sore throat. I suspect it's strep throat. Before you order your double latte, you will need to pick him up." The nurse has the power to cancel your wife's all important "Cut and Color" at the hair salon. No one, not the president, not the pope, has that kind of power, folks.

But their power extends far beyond this, of course. Nurses can strike fear in the hearts of moms, especially the young mothers. The ones who have one kid at school, two at home, and tend to be germ-phobic. You know the types—the "boy in a bubble" moms. Every subdivision has one. Nurses send home notices of horrible diseases and make clear that their adorable 8-year-old has been "exposed." The notices arrive on a bright yellow piece of paper, straight from the CDC. "A child at school has been diagnosed with the measles. Your child is at risk." The note recites other diseases that can compound the panic. Like pink eye, chicken pox, strep, mumps, whooping cough, head lice.

School nurses can trump teachers. Kids know this. The school nurse office is the last refuge from important tests little Johnny is not prepared to take. The office has a bed, pillows, blankets and a thermostat that can put Johnny in a Rumplestiltskin type of slumber for three days.

But anyone with this much power has to be good. And they are. They are part mother, part teacher, part doctor and all detective. There is no insurance, no paperwork. Kids walk in, cough, and get cured. If our President got smart, he would appoint a school nurse as head of FEMA. In two days she would turn things around.

For this column I interviewed the school nurse at my son's middle school. My son tends to get to know her during finals, if you know what I'm saying. This underpaid, overworked lady told me all kinds of stories. The most amusing ones were of the great lengths kids employ to fake sick. Everything from thermometers baked over a lamp to pretend vomiting. "Always the boys," she added. On an average day she will see anywhere from forty to sixty kids. One bad week she saw

120 students. Per day. In some schools the job description goes well beyond diagnosing sore throats and includes detecting child abuse and all kinds of other horrible things I'll leave for The Star's Metropolitan section.

So listen up moms—if caller ID says it's the school calling, cancel the Prairie Life yoga session. Little Johnny has strep. Mother's day out is mother's day in.

Published March 4, 2006

School fundraisers: Count me out.

As most parents know all too well, grade schools and fund raising go hand in hand. Whether it's promoted by the PTO or some overbearing principal seeking a slush fund for administrative boondoggles, it's a fact of life for most parents today.

Catholic schools have this down to a science. I know, trust me. My kids attend Catholic schools, and I'm the product of a Catholic education. There's something about hyperactive grade-school students dressed in uniforms that translates into a money-raising bonanza of heavenly proportions.

And though you won't find it in the New Testament, I suspect the first assignment Jesus gave to the apostles was to sell trash bags. Not much has changed since.

In my grade school out in western Kansas, St. Patrick's, Sister Mary Rose used all the tools in her arsenal: car raffles, magazine sales, bingo games, and the obligatory school carnival. If my hometown had more than two businesses, they would have also sold those annoying "Gold C" coupon books, too.

But all this was nothing compared with the annual candy sale. We sold chocolate almond bars that looked and were priced like they came from Fort Knox. I think back then they went for $2.50 a bar. It was a fascinating marketing plan: to entrust candy to sugar-obsessed second-graders with instructions to "sell now; collect later." At the school entrance, they constructed this giant thermometer with the sales goal at the top. And every morning Sister Mary Rose came on the PA to give us the daily updates right before the morning prayers. Brilliant.

In my children's school, they have just one fund-raiser in the fall: magazine sales. The school recently kicked off the campaign with an assembly in the gymnasium, a combination between a pep rally and religious revival. Organizers package prizes with a billion other promotions, and place grades and classes in competition with each other.

The highlight of this rally is the revelation of the prizes for the top sellers. It's never anything you can buy at the store, at least not without traveling to places such as Branson or Bagnell Dam in the Ozarks. This year's prizes include—honestly now—the Rainbow Monkey, Mini UFO Light, Hyper Scan Radio and Cyber Frog Phone. The fair market value of any of these prizes is about a dollar. Yet, my wife and I spent a hundred times that amount in magazines so our children could win the coveted Bubble Monkey—a 6-inch plastic primate that spits bubbles continuously.

When I was at St. Pat's, we sold everything door to door. Between St. Pat's and our cross-town rival, St. Rose, basically the entire city of Great Bend was one big child labor violation. Today, of course, no parent with a brain would let her son and daughter ring every door bell in three ZIP codes like we used to do. So that means the parents are the buyers.

Indeed, the instructional flier that my kids' school sent home with every child includes a "prospective customer list" so devoid of meaning that it even suggests students target "people you mow lawns for" as patrons. Wow. These fund-raising guys are obviously stuck in the '70s. Grade-school kids stopped mowing lawns 15 years ago, and our country hasn't been the same since.

Parents hate all this, of course. Because schools never sell anything that every household needs just one of. Never. Think about it. When was the last time you saw nuns running a car wash?

So my children's PTO had a great idea. The group put to the parents a choice: One final year of fund raising then switch to an annual assessment of all parents or continue to have pyramid-Ponzi selling schemes indefinitely. Magazines lost 350 to zero. So, the Keenan children have sold their last magazines. In the year 2010, our subscriptions to Catholic Digest will finally expire.

And to help us remember those wonderful times, we have bubbles circulating throughout our home. Courtesy of an adorable Bubble Monkey. Not available in stores.

Published December 7, 2002

All Boy High School Suits Keenan Just Fine

It's back to school time. This year our family has two sons going to High School. Both attending Rockhurst. This school has a solid academic reputation, but it has another distinction that my wife and I like a lot—the fact that for five days a week, the only women my sons will see will be those teaching their classes.

You see, I figure the probability of success for the Keenans boys goes up considerably by eliminating as many distractions as possible. All boys are prone to distraction, my boys especially so. Lets face it, girls are a distraction. Let me restate that.

What I mean is that girls are wonderful but in the same classroom as boys they have the *potential* to avert the boys' eyes from the chalkboard. And girls who appear 20 but dress like they are 10 can be more captivating than a discussion of the quadratic equations. And unless you just hatched from an egg you know that more young ladies are wearing less these days.

This is no knock on the public schools, mind you. Its just that sometimes in life parents get to make choices for their children. And for us, this one was an opportunity of a lifetime.

In my book, an all boys school will help ensure that discussion of the anatomy takes place entirely in biology class. An all boys school makes certain that the only organs working during class are those that play music. An all boys school guarantees they if my sons team up on a science project the experiments will be in accord with the textbook.

If they have to call a classmate to learn the homework assignment, I know the call will be short. Really short. Like "Dude. [long pause]. Got math? [long pause]. Cool. Thanks."

There are other benefits. I don't have to read and understand lengthy school policies governing public displays of affection, for example. Thirty years ago my high school was decidedly coed. Back then PDA meant something other than owning an Ipod. There was groping, grabbing and mashing. My entire freshman year all I did was stare.

At Rockhurst my sons take a vacation from the body sprays and other scented fragrances that fumigate our home on the weekends. I save a small fortune on the topical facial creams and Clearasil. Hair is far less important, so long as its short. This is Rockhurst, after all.

My sixteen year old doesn't care about his 'rent a wreck' car sitting in the parking lot. There are pep rallies but nothing led by perky petite coeds who get tossed up fifty feet by someone named Biff. Rockhurst has a dress code but no one bothers to test it. And every once in a while they have special days where my sons get to wear a white pressed shirt, tie and slacks. How refreshing.

They keep the testosterone bottled up until Friday night football, where most of the plays happen behind the bleachers. Rockhurst also has what they call "coed mixers" with schools like Sion and St. Teresa's. There the hormones go crazy. But these socials are more heavily chaperoned than family day at Leavenworth Penitentiary. At these functions the Axe fog rolls in and suffocates mosquitoes within a two mile radius of 95th and State Line.

Parents who enroll their daughters in single sex schools have all this figured out. They would say, I'm sure, that boys are a distraction. Studies have shown that separating boys from girls leads to better grades, more educational opportunities for both genders. Some coed schools have single sex math and science classes because students learn more in those environments.

So call the Keenans 'old school' when it comes to High School. We like it a lot.

Published August 20, 2005

3

Bernie Our Dog

Bernie is our family dog, and the most popular family member. She never talks back, she always welcomes you, and obeys the most simple commands. Bernie has no I-Pod and never makes any demands, except that I scratch her belly every morning. I would gladly trade three teenage boys for another Bernie. I would even throw in a couple cell phones and a generous calling plan.

Bernie's Day Out

I have written about our family dog, Bernie, from time to time. Bernie is a Wheaton Terrier, female. Don't ask me how she got a male's name. Strange things happen when left to a family vote. Anyway, Bernie is the most important member of the Keenan family and gets preferential treatment normally reserved for British Royalty. That's true of most pets. And in universe of great days that Bernie has enjoyed, what happened two weeks ago was in the top five. That's because we took her to the first "Doggie Dunk" at the Leawood City pool.

For two hours on a Tuesday night, the pool was opened to dogs. And they came. Over a hundred. But in the entire mix, as best I could tell, there was only one Bernie. One Wheaton, one dog whose last name was Keenan. And it showed.

This event was part Westminister dog show, part doggie Venice Beach, and all sniffing.

There were three pools. Each was chock full of canine eye candy. At one pool there was a contingent of labs and other retrievers. They were standing together near the edge of the deep end. They were reserved, poised. Some were showing off, retrieving tennis balls. Others just stood there, appearing as if they had just put away their cell phones trying to figure out where the next pool party was. Their owners were smug; their dogs were the best in show.

There was also an entire different segment of tiny, "yappy" dogs. These were the puppy mill rejects who somehow had slipped past the guy checking ID's at the door. Most needed a sedative—the owners, I mean. The dogs cried out for a flea dip and tick collar. These little fellas had no clue that in Darwin's equation they were two chromosomes removed from Critter Control.

And then there was Bernie. She walked among the minions and remained calm, composed, in control. Like Simba only better. Like Spuds McKenzie only taller. And then it happened.

The sniffing. First it was the goldens. One by one they walked up to Bernie and sniffed her up. And down. And up. Then came the labs. They would stand next to her, exchange glances, and then put the nose in action. Bernie, no doubt embarrassed by the shakedown, remained unruffled by all the attention. But it was incredible. Nordstroms' perfume counter has less sniffing. Bernie was clearly the catch. She had her weekly "cut and color" from the finest dog handlers, the Red Bridge Kennel. She was the only Wheaton in sight.

The parade of dogs continued for a couple minutes. I figured it was harmless, since Bernie was single. I also figured that since she had been 'fixed' it was unlikely my nine year old daughter would see any intruders get too frisky, if you know what I'm saying.

And then out of nowhere, came another dog. It was a small, very unattractive dog. He couldn't look Bernie in the eye. His owner had no footstool. The dog promptly put its nose to work.

I asked the owner "what kind of dog is that?"

"It's a pug" she said.

"Great," I said to myself. A pug right now is fantasizing about hooking up with the greatest dog on the planet. Like Mini Me hitting on Lady Diana. I tugged on the leash. Pug boy was history.

Two seconds later Bernie was staring at a huge black poodle. It had the typical big poodle hair cut—puff ball here, puff ball there, like Edward Scissorhands went insane. This dog was ugly. Small poodles I can deal with. This dog was huge. He (she?) had some bling bling, jumped around like he/she needed some decaf, and of course, sniffing. Other dogs were running from him/her. *Running away.* I'm not making this up. My daughter saw trouble and quickly took Bernie to the slide.

Next we came across another dog of some unrecognizable breed. I asked the owner, "what kind of dog is that?"

"It's a Labradoodle," she said, all puffed up and proud.

I shook my head. This poor thing didn't know whether to chase a stick or chase a dog. This dog's issues were about to migrate to her nose, and that spelled trouble for you know who.

I would have none of it.

And so once the shakedown ended, Bernie was finally able to relax in the wading pool—with the only companion she really wanted.

My daughter.

Published September 17, 2005

The family dog and allergies: one more Keenan crisis

I was having a bad day at work when my wife called.

"The vet said that Bernie might have allergies. That explains why she is having ear infections." Then she hung up. Bernie—the Wheaten Terrier—had a medical crisis. My day just got worse. And my wallet suddenly felt lighter.

A sick dog is worse than a sick child. The dog is not just a member of the family—she owns the family in the palm of her paw.

Dog is God spelled backwards, and in our home on such matters, my kids tend to be dyslexic. Bernie is the only occupant welcomed into every bedroom in the house at any time of the day or night. When not plopped on one of the beds at night, she lies on the first floor like a throw rug with legs. We step over her gingerly. The only doghouse is a metaphorical one whose only occupant is me.

I knew full well that the notion of Bernie suffering would consume my wife and children. Seconds later I was shaking my head in disbelief. The words "allergy" and "Bernie" go together like "Donald Trump" and "great hair."

This is a dog that has spent the last five years making living arrangements among tulips, grass, and weeds of various types. She is impervious to snow, rain, water, and underground fences. The only time she has coughed involved barking up a toad. Food allergies are unthinkable as well. Her track record with pepperoni pizza, sweet-and-sour shrimp, tacos, chicken salad and fruit salads is most impressive. Virtually anything you can serve on a plate or drop beneath the table will vanish in seconds. For her, the greatest buffet in the world would consist of all the food groups, served by Sunshine, the family cat.

I knew that once this diagnosis hit home my children would demand vets trained at the Mayo clinic. My kids would suddenly be obsessed with pollen counts. I could see it now: "Dad, Bernie sneezed. Should I call 911?" Itching and scratching would be grounds for relocating to Sun City.

I connected the dots. Bernie had two infections in her ear. Both required expensive drops. From my early parenting days, I knew repeated ear infections can lead to pharmacy bills of obscene proportions, then ear tubes, hearing tests, then speech therapy.

With Bernie, it was clear where this path would lead me: bankruptcy, divorce and then taking up residence under a bridge in the Grandview triangle.

That evening, when I arrived home, Bernie was obviously not affected by this devastating development. She met me at the front door as if I had been rescued from a deserted island. After attacking me, she rolled over for me to scratch parts of her body only I can reach.

Bernie knows when I've had a bad day. And on this day, I half expected her to speak the voice of Dean Jones and offer to fix me a bourbon on the rocks.

At dinner she lay below the dinner table and waited for the scraps to come her way. Which they did. And at bedtime she curled up on my son Tommy's bed like she owned the place. Which she does.

Poor thing. She will never be the same.
Neither will I.

Published April, 2004.

4

Boy Scouts

In small towns like Great Bend, Boy Scouts was enormously popular. My two brothers and I spent half our teenage years living in a tent. And so when the good Lord gave me three sons of my own, Boy Scouts was the one thing that was non-negotiable. Little did I know, but it would give me a lifetime of material for my columns.

Pinewood Derby adventures come full circle with son's success

By most objective standards, I'm probably not a very good parent. My failings could fill this entire newspaper and indeed have in previous columns. I'm tough when I should be forgiving and forgiving when I should be tough. The red flags for my flaws were apparent many years ago, when our sons showed their penchant for "drop to the ground" temper tantrums at obscure places like Christmas Mass.

In contrast, my mom and dad seemed to do most things right. They raised five kids and never played it safe. They constantly tossed my brothers and sisters in harm's way. We won some, lost more and learned that life is not fair and complaining about it does not make it more equitable. Now in case you think I've become the next Dr. Phil, stick with me for a moment. I'm getting to my point.

And that point is the Pinewood Derby. That little five-inch block of wood is a metaphor for much about parenting—and life. That piece of lumber embodies the hopes, dreams and worldly expectations of a boy—a boy who believes that his dad is invincible and that any undertaking uniting father with son cannot possibly fail. Until it does.

Like me, my dad had three sons, all in Scouts, all needing Pinewood cars. And like me, my dad had little time and less talent to build anything. He owned no saws, drills, hammers or even nails. If necessity is the mother of invention, my dad was Mother Hubbard.

He taught me that steak knives are more useful for carving wood than filets. That a fishing tackle box contains almost everything you need to achieve the desired weight of five ounces. That brown carpet can swallow a couple pounds of graphite without even a hint of stain. And that you can complete three weeks of work on the night before the weigh-in. His makeshift approach did nothing to dampen my expectations. We never took home any trophies or ribbons. But every year we kept trying.

A generation later I have remained largely faithful to that legacy. This month my fifth-grade son, Robert, raced his last car in his Cub Scout Pinewood Derby. Between him and his two brothers, our family has made 12 cars over eight years.

In the early years, it was one misadventure after another. And we had frustration, disappointment and tears. But every year we got better. I picked up some tips my dad never appreciated, learning that when wheels rub against the chassis, the odds of your son holding the championship trophy are long. When his finished car rolls in a semicircle on your kitchen floor, those odds roughly double. And the digital postal scale at Hy-Vee is critical to achieving the perfect weight of five ounces.

And when the derby arrived on the last Friday in January, our efforts came full circle. Among 70 competitors, the final two cars included the one belonging to a fifth-grader named Keenan. Second place. Meaning his car will run one more time, in the countywide Pinewood Derby contest.

And when my son's final car runs its final race, we will retire it in his bedroom, in the same way his brothers have. Each one has my son's name taped to the underside, assigned at the weigh-in. Each one will have a story—each one an embodiment of hopes, dreams and expectations. Some realized, others dashed. Each one symbolizes a special time in their young lives, when we lived and learned and came to recognize the value of taking a chance on a block of wood, just like another father and his sons did 30 years ago.

Published January 2001.

It isn't a camp-out without rain

Americans love to camp. And buy camping stuff. Americans, in fact, bought more than a billion dollars of camping gear last year.

I like to camp, too. But only under sane conditions. Like blue skies, cool weather with no threat of rain for at least 30 days. With a golden arches close enough to see from my tent.

As a kid, I was a Boy Scout and camped all the time. But it was different then. I was young and stupid. Subsequently, I developed a fondness for warm beds, fluffy pillows and shake-shingle roofs. When I travel—which is often—I enjoy the comforts of room service and the concierge lounge. But God blessed me with three sons, and one day I did what my dad did some 30 years ago: I signed them up for Scouts.

That event by itself complicated my life a bit. It's when I agreed to be a leader, however, that things got interesting.

Now, there is much good in camping with your sons. And when it's combined with Boy Scouts, there is an even greater good. That said, let me make a few observations. For starters, at some point someone declared that camping requires just enough equipment for you to pretend that you never left your home in the first place. That means packing your car—no matter its size—to the absolute limits.

I figure Lewis and Clark traveled the country with some boats and some horses or mules. They became true American heroes. But if they made that trip today, they'd need 15 semis and a cruise ship.

Sporting goods stores contribute to all this, telling you that you should never camp without a water-purification system and special flashlights you place on your head like a coal miner.

Every campsite has a fire, of course. But because the Scouts often camp in designated campgrounds, the firewood is picked over like Wal-Mart on Christmas Eve. Consequently, you end up sending the Scouts deep enough into the trees to permit them to interact at a close personal level with poison ivy. Inevitably, your grand plans of starting the fire with flint and steel are quickly converted to matches, paper towels and lighter fluid.

But no matter what else happens during my camping trips, there is one sure thing: rain. I don't care what the forecast says. It will rain when I camp. Guaranteed. Sometimes it's just harmless sprinkles. But often, the rain comes down sideways. Six of my last seven campouts, it has rained. My wife thinks it's a message from God.

The very first camp-out of my Scout leadership career was this thing called the "Camporee." I think that's French for "impending disaster." They bring Scouts from all over together for a weekend camp-out. It's a date planned months in advance, rain or shine. In 1998, it was held at Smithville Lake, and apparently every adult but me had watched the Weather Channel. As we met in the church parking lot, multiple dads began employing the "drive-by drop-off."

It was like in those movies when everyone knows something bad is going to happen except the guy about to be killed, and everybody but him starts to walk backward, first slowly then running. Over and over again, I was left standing there with little Johnny, his sleeping bag, and a backpack full of water-purification equipment.

Around 10:30 that fall night, my fourth-grade Webelos went from snuggling in their Lion King sleeping bags to re-enacting the final scene from "Platoon." Tents blew away, lightning struck all around us, and water soaked everything. The weather man said it was a microburst. I called it hell.

I had payback, however, on those parents who had abandoned me. I enjoyed the privilege of dropping off the children dripping wet on their parents' porches at midnight.

The boys handled the situation fine, but four years of counseling have done little to heal my mental anguish. So if you enjoy the great outdoors and have plans to camp anytime soon, do something smart. Call me first. Because if I'm also camping, the drought is coming to a quick end.

Published October 2003

Scout camp a rite of passage

Summertime, for many kids, means camp. These days the camp business is big business. My kids have done their share of various camps. But in my book, for my sons, Boy Scout camp has no peer. And the Scout camp of choice in our home is the H. Roe Bartle Scout Reservation, 80 miles southeast of Kansas City, near Osceola, Mo.

For the next week and half, my two sons are calling that little spot home. Camp Sawmill, Locust Campsite. Troop 396. Church of the Nativity.

Scout camp strips away the clutter that distracts today's youth. It's cultural detox for today's teenager. For nine days, they function without the Disney Channel, their Game Cube, PlayStation, and AOL instant messaging. When your bed is a sleeping bag-adorned cot and your tent flap is your window to the world, your perspective on life changes. The day starts with reveille and ends with taps. And one of the most important things all day is the flag ceremony.

Scout camp is where your teenager no longer finds your presence embarrassing. Where he wears the uniform and scarf without being disagreeable. Where he notices the moon, the Big Dipper, fossil formations in the rocks, and appreciates the difference between a garter snake and a copperhead. Where an early morning thunderstorm is nature's own symphony. Where he willingly hikes for two miles to a town called Iconium that really is nothing more than a country store. Just to order an ice cream float and sit on the front porch and talk to his friends. And laugh. A lot.

But Scout camp is more than simply boys interacting with the outdoors. It's an environment that rewards achievement and recognizes that the best role models are the boys themselves. It also serves to break down cliques and social boundaries that form when the boys are in more familiar surroundings.

For me as a young Scout, Bartle was not an option. The Scouts from western Kansas went to a place called Camp Kanza. It was near Hutchinson, which is near absolutely nothing. In mid-July at camp it was 110 degrees in the shade with no shade. The terrain was like a lunar landscape. No matter; we had a blast.

Bartle, of course, is the vision of its namesake. The Boy Scouts acquired the first property in the fall of 1929, and the first Scouts camped there in 1930. Bartle became a Scout executive in the 1920s and began devising the Tribe of Mic-O-Say to campers, which is an honor program for Scouts and their leaders. All of this from a man who had no sons and was not in Boy Scouts himself. The camp's success today is due as much to his vision as it is to the great adult leaders who give of their time and talents to the summer programs.

I'm a believer in Boy Scouts and their camps. It's hard not to admire any organization that teaches boys to be men and has a track record of over 90 years of success. An organization that embraces a simple motto: Be prepared.

This week over a 1,000 Scouts are joining my sons at Bartle. And on Wednesday afternoon, my boys will return home to an anxious mother, brother and sister. And when they do, they will be wiser, more mature, and I believe, better boys as result of their 10 days at Bartle Scout reservation.

Published June 14, 2003

Out-of-control Cub Scouts, demure Brownies

My daughter Maggie recently joined Brownies. For those unacquainted with the group, Brownies is an introduction to Girl Scouts for girls in first, second and third grades.

Maggie is in first grade and has a brother in Cub Scouts, Robert. Cub Scouts, for boys in grades 2-5, is the prelude to Boy Scouts.
In less than a year, I have already learned a lot about the differences between Cubs and Brownies.

Both organizations like to use grade-school kids in massive fund-raising schemes, but that's where the similarities end.
Brownies, you see, sell cookies that everyone wants. Cub Scouts sell popcorn that no one wants. Brownies are walking, talking, selling machines. Cub Scouts couldn't sell their popcorn in a movie theater.

The meetings are completely different too. Brownie meetings involve delightful 8-year-olds sitting still and engaging in fine-motor tasks, such as making puppets, coloring and storytelling. The girls are polite and patient. They share snacks, assist in cleaning up, and hug their leaders at the end of the meeting.

Cub Scouts, on the other hand, really don't have meetings. Instead, the boys run around—chasing each other nonstop, screaming, breaking valuables, turning snacks into weapons and harassing everyone in sight.

On the other hand, the uniforms are very similar. Both are partial to beads and other small objects easy to misplace at critical moments. Both require extensive sewing with complicated instructions about where you place each patch. But Brownie patches favor designs with rainbows, flowers and hearts while Cub Scout patches favor arrows, hatchets, matches and bonfires. Brownie uniforms are easily available, sold at many stores. Cub Scout uniforms are available at only one place: the exclusive "Scout Shop" at Interstate 435 and Holmes Road.

The organizations also differ with regard to adult leadership. Based on my experience, Brownie leaders are in abundant supply. Moms wear the uniform proudly and accessorize it to be stylish. Such is not the case when it comes to Cub Scout leaders. Trust me, I'm what they call the "Cubmaster."

A Cubmaster oversees several groups of Scouts, and you get the job when you show up late for an important Scout meeting. Finding leaders for Cub Scouts is like locating Osama bin Laden. When I start dialing for leaders, I block my caller ID or else parents won't answer the phone.

Both types of Scouts take field trips. Brownies like craft shops, puppet shows and jewelry design stores. Cub Scouts like to go to police stations, fire stations, jails and fireworks factories.
Brownies have a disdain for competition among the girls. Cub Scouts embrace it. Think Pinewood Derby—an event that turns otherwise passive suburban fathers into rabid, compulsive woodworking freaks.

The contrasts are never greater, however, than when the time comes for something like Scout Sunday. Scout Sunday is one day when both genders of Scouts come together and celebrate their faith. Just last week we had our Scout Sunday in our parish. At the end of the Mass, the priest invited all the Scouts up to the altar.

There, they stood and sang the final hymn. The girls sang passionately and stood in perfect formation as proud mothers snapped constant photos. Their uniforms were pressed, with matching bows, socks and shoes. The Cub Scouts sported wrinkled uniforms with scarves the boys tied around their necks like a noose. Many had no scarves, and some had no uniforms at all. All dressed themselves in the back seat of the van on the way to church.

While the Brownies looked as if they should have halos, the Cubs wrestled, pushed and shoved each other—entirely oblivious to the gasps of the congregation sitting in front of them. Few parents dared to waste film on these boys. Indeed, no parent dared to claim them.

I give my time to this organized chaos because there is some good here—in Cub Scouts as well as Brownies. I know it because I grew up in Scouting some 30 years ago. Even today, those years form some of the fondest memories from my youth.

That's something I try to remember when I find myself peeling third-graders off the cafeteria floor during Scout meetings.

Published February 15, 2003

Adventures in the New Mexico wilderness

Today's article is my postscript from two weeks at Philmont Scout Reservation outside Cimarron, N.M. For me, it was unlike anything I have experienced in my 46 years. Without question, it was the most physically demanding "vacation" I've taken. But it was so much more than that.

Philmont represents over 100,000 acres of mountainous land donated to the Boy Scouts through the generosity of Waite Phillips of Phillips 66 fame. And for over 50 years, it has been the ultimate Boy Scout adventure. You hike with a loaded backpack and function without cell phones, laptops and BlackBerries. The boys drop the Xbox controls and pick up a compass, a large map of back trails, elect a crew leader and navigate 75 miles over mountains, across streams, through forests and eventually to the campsites designated each night.

If they get lost—which is common—they find their way. The dads assist the boys only if asked. Philmont is truly "old school"—a landscape devoid of cell phone towers, condominium developments and roads. In their place are meadows that punctuate thick forests. Vistas so beautiful that no columnist or photographer could do them justice. Trails through forests that you would never notice unless you were standing on top of them.

Five stories are worth sharing.

■ The Hair. Backcountry hiking and long hair do not mix well. Yet 15-year-olds worship their long locks. But on the night before we left, I watched in sheer amazement as all eight boys decided to get a haircut. But this was no light trim. They wanted the full nine yards—the buzz cut. When it was all done, the grass looked like the Marines enlisted Rapunzel.

■ The Bear. Philmont has black bears—and elaborate procedures to ensure no bears gain access to anything that hikers bring into the forest. Food primarily, but then anything else that smells—toothpaste, soap, film, sunscreen, you name it. We used "bear bags"—hung well above the ground to store the forbidden items. But few people attest to actually seeing a bear. Early in our venture, I inquired of other campers we encountered on the trail, "Did you see any bears?" The reply, consistently, was the same: "Nope." So by day five, I was convinced that this bear thing was on par with Big Foot and Roswell alien sightings. But all that changed on day six.

I was getting water for dinner not far from our campsite when a fellow camper standing next to me uttered five words that I will never forget: "Holy (expletive) there's a bear." And when I looked to my left, two things instantly came to mind. First, bears are real. Second, I need clean underwear.

This bear was huge, five to six feet high on all fours. It stared directly at me and growled. I did not blink. I did not back down. I stood firm. The next thing I knew I was found in the fetal position near some bushes. The bear went up a tree and stayed there long enough for the eight boys in our group to confirm for themselves that, yes, Philmont has bears.

■ The water. For several days the only water available was from a stream. Watching streams flow is one thing. Drinking it is another. Even when "treated," this water was like an amusement park for floating sea monkeys, leeches and other members of the animal kingdom. The consumers were boys who at home refuse to share cups with siblings due to bogus germ phobias. Philmont changed that. Our Philmont ranger, who was with us for the first two days, instructed us how to treat the water. If we did it wrong, we were at risk of diarrhea "for life." (OK, so he wasn't a doctor; we still believed him.)

■ The bat. These eight boys spend too much time playing video games—no revelation there. But very quickly they learned that their hands could do more than manipulate a joystick. A piece of wood from the forest and a plastic football led to an intense baseball rivalry with a group of scouts from Michigan who camped near us. They played these games in sloping, picturesque meadows. They were every bit as intense and at times as skillful as anything you would see at Johnson County 3&2. These scouts did so much more: cooking, carrying food, water, enduring rain, hail (four inches), lightning and temperatures below freezing on two mornings.

■ The talk. The boys rediscovered the lost art of conversation. Words like "dude" and "stupid" evaporated from their vocabulary, replaced with terms like "please" and "good morning." And on the evening of day nine, when my two sons crawled into the tent we called home for two weeks, my older son said to me, "This was fun, Dad. I'm glad we came."

I knew then this was more than a vacation. It was an adventure of life. Probably exactly what Mr. Phillips envisioned so many years ago. And for his gift, and the efforts of the Boy Scouts who have preserved his legacy, I am most grateful.

Published August 13, 2005

Photographs

Matt, Marty and the one that didn't get away.

Failures of the rhythm method.

Sister Kate, Mom, Aunt Dottie, Dad, 1972.

My mother's parents—Jacob and Olga Goering, with Mom and Dad.

Easter 1966

Matt Keenan, Bill Niederee, John Holt, circa 1969. The makings of three Eagle Scouts.

(photo courtesy of Charlotte Holt.)

Larry, Mona and kids, circa 1963

My wife Lori and her soul mate.

My siblings, my father L-R:
Marty, Beth, Matt, Kate, Timothy and Dad 2006

Matt Keenan, Bill Niederee, John Holt. First Communion, circa 1967.

Webelos Camp, July 2004, Camp Naish, 110 degrees in the shade with no shade.
Keenan with Dan McCord, fellow scout leader, Pack 3096, and an unnamed adult leader about to go code blue. As far we know, no scouts died on this campout.

Connor and Tommy Keenan, Philmont back country, July 2005.

Dad, and my step-mom, Patti Degner, July 2005.

Why God gave us daughters. Maggie, Connor, Tommy and Robert Keenan, circa 1998.

5

Sports

My most popular columns are about sports. There is so much material. Here are my best.

Bad News Bears Comes to Leawood

Walter Mathau's greatest move ever was the Bad News Bears. That movie title has become code for the collection of kids who can't hit, throw or run. All on one team.

All good stories have a great beginning. This one is no exception. Parents know all too well that there comes a time in sports when neighborhood teams split up, and suddenly nice boys have no team. When coaches want to 'take it up a level' and rosters are tossed to the wind. This is no criticism of any parent or any coach. It's a natural evolution of most teams. That happened to my son Robert this Spring. His team split up, the coach retired, and suddenly he was orphaned. So I had a team of one player.

So I had some positions to fill. I had two criteria. First, you had to be a F.O.R.—friend of Robert. Second, you had to be able to swim. Because post game pool parties would be the most important thing all season.

Now this was a rec team. No tournaments. No practices in 110 degree heat. No special coaches shorts with three snap buttons on the front. But rec teams are not insulated from the challenges that come with playing at a higher level. It was the first full season of "player pitch." Instructing a nine year old to throw a baseball from a distance of 45 feet into a strike zone about the size of postage stamp is not just difficult. It's impossible. The result is walks, hit batters, pitched balls flying behind, over and under batters.

Hitting is another world of challenges. Someone once said that hitting a ball with a bat is the hardest thing to do in all sports. I believe it. Michael Jordan is the greatest athlete to play any sport. But when he tried to play baseball, he made the Titanic look seaworthy. And then there's finding a catcher. The only boy that likes to play catcher is one who has never done it in July in a dust storm. The knee guards, chest protector, face mask and glove weigh about 100 pounds. My catcher weighs fifty.

Yes, there were some things about our season that I did not enjoy. Every league has a coach who needs a wake-up call. It's the coach who thought our game was game 7 of the World Series. You know the type. The guy whose veins pop out on his forehead when his player strikes out with the bases loaded. The guy who thinks scoring 30 runs against us is worthy of a resume revision. The guy whose uniform extends from head to toe. Whose lineup was created on an Excel spreadsheet with footnotes and bold type.

Other than these issues, baseball is a breeze. In our first game, I told one of the boys to play left field. He looked at me—and honestly now—said "where's that?" "In left field" I said. He stood there, looking anxious. I pointed the way. Off he ran. We had other adventures. Stealing bases comes to mind. Kids love to do anything that uses the word "steal." I shared the steal sign—very simple—hand across the chest. They sat there, stared intently. "Everyone got it? Nods across the bench.

But something happens to a 9 year old's brain when he gets on base. Cerebral functions slow. Nerve synapse stop firing. They go brain dead. After four innings, I changed my plan. The steal sign was simple: I yelled at the top of lungs: STEAL! There were other adventures. One boy arrived at game time with his pants on backwards. Swear. We also had players arrive 10 minutes into the game and wanted to know why they were batting last.

This story has a happy ending. No, it doesn't end like the Bad News Bears. No we didn't rally in the bottom of the 6th inning to win the championship. Our season ended with a loss. A bad defeat. But no one cried. No one cared. Most of the kids didn't even knew the score. We were off to the neighborhood pool for the post game party.

So for a group of boys who gave me so much, I wanted to give them something in return. And tokens or trophies just won't cut it. So my parting gift is unusual. Something worthy of the scrapbook. For the Sluggers, Robert, Kevins 1,2, and 3, Tim, Anthony, Toms 1 and 2, Raymond, Alex, Ethan, this article is for you.

Published July 2003

Sluggers bring back baseball fun

There was a time, long ago, when every grade school had its own sandlot baseball team. And every grade school boy played on it. In the '60s and '70s, countless kids passed the time on summer days playing pickup baseball games. They filled the lineup with ghost runners and other things passed down from older brothers.

In my western Kansas town, Homerun Derby was the time-honored tradition. The chain-link fence was about a hundred feet from home and everyone had a shot to "park it" as we used to say. Back then, we rode bikes to practice and carried a wood bat signed by Babe Ruth. Never mind that he'd been dead for 30 years. We did other crazy things, like drink water from a garden hose and mow yards. Seasons lasted 10 games, and after each game you went to Dairy Queen for a slushie.

But between 1974 and today, something happened to youth baseball. It ceased to be sandlot. Someone decided baseball had to be serious. That you had to play 40 games and compete in tournaments in cities like Omaha.

Coaches formed premier teams. That meant good players got cherry-picked and bad players got cut. Every game players were not just competing against their opponent, they were competing for a roster spot.

Equipment got complicated too. Kids started accumulating things like bat bags and batting gloves. Coaches followed suit. Neighborhood teams began to go the way of the dodo bird. And baseball as a sport, not surprisingly, began to suffer. Surveys reflect that of all the team sports, baseball is losing players faster than any other.
Our Leawood neighborhood was not impervious to all this. So in 2003 through a set of circumstances I hope to never repeat, I found myself coaching the school baseball team. And on the day of the Blue Valley sign-ups, four of my best players got "recruited away" by another coach. That day was one I would like to forget.

So that weekend I sat down with my fourth-grade son Robert and cobbled together a roster of new players. Experience, and talent level, was not a consideration. And that summer the Nativity Sluggers, not surprisingly, went 1-11. The next year we doubled our win total.

Yet, somewhat to my surprise, everyone was having fun. None of the players knew or cared about our standings. Any my wife reminded me this team would never have a problem that curses other teams: No rival coach would steal these players.

And so in spring 2005, something quite unexpected happened. In early March, while practicing at a neighborhood ball diamond I noticed a boy ride his bike to the field. He lived nearby. But this was not just any kid.

This was the best pitcher, the best hitter in Nativity Parish school. One of the four players who abruptly left our team for greener pastures. He also happened to be my son's best friend.

As I pitched batting practice he walked to the outfield and started shagging balls. Later he picked up a bat. Ten minutes later he was still hitting pitches that were landing in neighboring subdivisions. I quickly learned that he quit his premier team. In fact, he was not on any team. And so at the end of practice I did what any good coach at that point: I took him to Sonic. There I ordered the usual—chili cheese dogs and a Sonic Blast.

When I dropped him off at his house, I played closer: "We have room for another player if you are interested." His response was quick. "I'll play."

And then one addition became two. Yes, the second best player in the school. And the Sluggers won games we used to lose. Kids at the bottom of the lineup got better. Kids at the top got a lot better. Parents came to games in droves and brought brothers, sisters, neighbors, friends. Like the Royals. Only fewer errors. And we made many return visits to Sonic.

And no we didn't play 30 games, we played 15. But when the season was over we went from worst to almost first in the Blue Valley League. So this summer, I'm happy to say, that in one city, one neighborhood, sandlot baseball is back.

Kansas City, meet the seventh-grade Nativity Sluggers.

Published June 3, 2006

Moms, sports and safety gear: trouble.

Moms, generally speaking, are safety freaks when it comes to their children. And so it is natural to expect moms to buy the latest, greatest safety gear when it concerns protecting little Johnny on the sports field.

And when the sport is little league baseball, it reaches a new level altogether. This is the sport with one very hard ball thrown by wild pitchers, metallic bats swung in broad circles with teammates standing close by, and ground balls just waiting to take an unexpected bounce. So moms invest in the mouth guards, helmets and the like.

But there is one piece of safety gear that poses special challenges for mom and little Johnny. ***The cup***. A triangular molded device that keeps Johnny's mid section safe, a plastic piece that little Johnny's sisters might mistake for a stylish serving bowl.

The cup is one safety device that has not changed one bit over the last thousand years. It remains a piece of injection molding that has the flexibility of titanium steel.

I have some familiarity with all this. When I was playing catcher for the St. Pat's Knights in 1969, Great Bend, Kansas had one sporting goods store—Phillips Sporting Goods. The owner was like 90 years old and couldn't hear a sonic boom if it happened behind his head. And the day when my dad took me down there to be fitted is a day I'd love to forget.

Dad was yelling loud and kept repeating the same question: "my son needs a cup." Mr Phillips: "How old is he?" Dad: "He's 10. Probably take a small." "What?" "He needs a small." Phillips: "He needs balls? Those are isle 5." Dad: "No, he's small. I think. I'm not sure." This went on for a couple minutes while other customers pretended to be occupied inspecting croquet sets.

Eventually I got the one size—the only size they carried—adult large—and then tried to act normal. I couldn't run, throw or hit. Other than that, I looked like Roy Hobbs. Eventually I did what my teammates did—I ditched it behind St. Pats ball diamond. Some toddler probably picked it up took it home and told his mom "look mom, a gas mask."

So fast forward 35 years. Not much as changed, of course. And I care about all this because I coach a sixth grade baseball team—the world famous Nativity Sluggers. My players are 11.

I work hard to get them ready to make the big play, the key hit. But a couple of moms are making my job difficult.

Some of my players have "sizing issues." You can pick these kids out of a crowd. They walk like they their moms dropped an Encyclopedia Britannica down their pants. But good luck raising this with their moms: I can see it now—"Coach said my cup was the wrong size." Two hours later I'm in the county jail trying to hire Michael Jackson's attorney.

So now you know that our win/loss record hardly tells the story of our team. That victories and defeats mean almost nothing to the moms of the Slugger boys. What is important is that when our season is measured based on injuries to these future Hall of Famers, we are undefeated. And that probably won't change anytime soon.

Published June 30, 2005

Coaching basketball for dads: The good, the bad, the ugly

In my book, every dad, at some point in his life, needs to coach a sports team. Any team would count but I give special marks to those who take on the "non-premier" type of team. Where the players have no idea what the word "tryout" means. Coaching these teams shapes your view of life unlike anything else. If someone ran for president whose resume including coaching a sandlot baseball team, he'd get my vote and money. He'd lose, of course, because he would be too nice. But I'd still vote for the guy.

Coaches have a special place in heaven. I know this. God told me so one hot July day in 2002. The Leawood Bad News Bears got slaughtered by the kids from early puberty school in Overland Park. The score was like a billion to zero.

I was in the dumps, staring at the heavens while my wife drove me home. She tried to pick me up. "You are a good coach. These are good kids with great parents." She paused. "Your team is getting better. It is." I looked over. "Tell me how." She paused. The car became dead silent. Crickets began their mating call. Eventually she reached for the car radio and fiddled with the dial.

Three years later God answered my prayers. That same team went from worst to first, but I'll save that for another column.

So anyway, this morning I got coaching on the brain. You see, while you are reading this in the comfort of your kitchen/bedroom/Starbucks/car, I'm in a 55 degree gym ten miles from my house trying to coach the Nativity seventh-grade CYO basketball team to our third victory in two seasons. CYO is the Catholic league, and it's not too bad, all in all. Before tip-off we hold hands and pray. After tip-off, the Lord's prayer leaves the gym, if you know what I mean.

But in the course of two seasons of basketball, I've learned a couple things. Basketball is harder to coach than all the other sports combined. Winter does strange things to kids. I can't explain it. For starters, in the gym they go crazy. Last year we practiced alongside one of the Nativity girls' team. The contrasts were incredible. The girls arrived early, did organized calisthenics, and raised their hands if they needed something. ("Is it OK if I go to the bathroom?") If there was a foul, the girls hugged and apologized. Our team, well, you get the picture.

I figured a couple other things out. Today's kids learn basketball from video games. So naturally they want to do two things. Dunk the ball or sink a half-court shot. Since most kids who play Xbox all day have difficulty "achieving verticality" (coach speak for jumping), dunking is out. So that leaves the half-court shot. Which they practice. Endlessly. Followed by the over-the-head shots, backward shots and behind-the-backboard shots. All of which require an audience of their teammates.

Another thing I learned: When you give permission to foul, it's open season for the kind of hostility they want to practice on their kid sister. They love plays that use the word "steal," "press" and "pick."

Baseball is nothing like this sport. It's slow. Coaches can plan and anticipate problems. You can lay things out. Basketball happens in a second and it's over. But both sports have some things in common, however. They both rely heavily on the "held back" kids and those that get facial hair at age 5. These guys always show up against my teams. In baseball they are the pitchers and catchers. In basketball they play everything. My basketball team has played against kids who are on a growth pattern to make Wilt look shrimpy.

So this year I figured it out. I recruited the big kid from the class. Never mind that he's never played basketball. He is unskilled at dribbling or shooting but really good at something else that makes him quite valuable to his team: shaving.

Published January 7, 2006

Soccer and fruit: a combination that must be stopped

This week I decided that I'm just as qualified as Dr. Phil and Oprah to offer advice to moms and dads about parenting. Oprah has never raised a child, or even been married. Dr. Phil has children, but he obviously never raised them because he is on television all the time. Dear Abby has passed on to give advice to the big man upstairs. So from time to time I'm going to tackle various topics and dispense my tidbits for improving and simplifying our lives.

Today's topic: soccer.

I have a real problem with this sport, and making it go away would significantly improve my life. My wife loves the sport, of course. Moms love any sport that does not require helmets with warnings in bold type: "Your son may die playing this game."

It's the soccer rules that have always bothered me. For example, "offsides" is a term applicable to 400-pound linemen, not some 90-pound weakling named Diego who wears really short shorts. The "no hands" thing troubles me too. Telling 9-year-olds they must play a game where they can't touch the ball is against the laws of nature. But I digress. The real problem I have has less to do with the game and more to do with another tradition inextricably bound up with this "sport."

Moms, follow with me here: It's Saturday morning. You have successfully located the shin guards, the jersey, the water bottle, the size 4 ball, the special cleats, the correct field (No. 14, not No. 4) and a parking spot. If you are like me, you have arrived plenty early—halfway through the first half—and pointed your daughter to her game. And then it hits you. That panic that works in tandem with your morning Starbucks.

THE DRINK AND ORANGE SCHEDULE! It's either your turn or it's not. You don't know but fear the worst. You sit in panic and scan the sidelines for any sign or suggestion that it's your day. You had the schedule, but then games were snowed out, rescheduled, rained out and then finally played at some field 10 miles from your home at 8 a.m.

Briefly, you contemplate a mad dash to the grocery store. There is no game clock—half time (a.k.a. orange exchange) could be two or 20 minutes away. It's hopeless. Go to Plan B: Pretend someone else had that duty. If you are confused, so are most other parents. Make another parent feel responsible by starting up the conversation "I'm glad it wasn't my day for oranges." Then quickly duck out to avoid follow-up Q & A.

So parents, listen up: This is where I strike pure genius. From this day forward, parents are relieved of this ridiculous burden. Millions of kids play soccer. That means this stupid tradition afflicts millions more parents.
Until now.

Kids play football, baseball, basketball, golf, paintball and PS2 just fine without littering the sidelines with orange peels. Some guy named Gerard in Paris conspired with the French orange growers and started this tradition a thousand years ago.
A guy named Keenan is going to stop it.

So parents, let the word go forth around the world: From this date forward no oranges, no post-game drinks, no schedule you lose and find a billion times, no stress. Attend little Johnny's soccer game, relax in your captain's chair, read The Star, and watch not a minute of the action. How refreshing.

Next on my hit list: Why baseball pants should be black, not white; banning coaches' gifts; and whatever else annoys me in the next month. Stay tuned.

Published April 2004

The soccer gods must be crazy

About 25 years ago Hollywood released a movie called "The Gods Must Be Crazy." It was about an African bushman who gets hit on the head with a bottle of Coke tossed from a passing airplane. The natives thought it was a gift from the gods. It became a treasured artifact until everyone started fighting over it. They eventually tossed it over some cliff and with the bottle went the plot.

But the title was great. And from time to time I think about that notion—that someone from above has gone insane.

Recently I was watching my fourth grade daughter's soccer game. I was having a pleasant time until another parent informed me that the next day, a Sunday morning, they were having a "tryout" for next year's team.

At that moment, I thought of those bushmen. Because Sunday morning sporting events are the worst idea ever created. I really dislike Sunday morning sporting events. Correction: I hate Sunday morning games. In fact I hate anything on a Sunday morning that does not involve church, a newspaper and a remote.

God made the earth in six days and rested on Sunday. Can't we learn something from that? Honestly, isn't there enough time from noon to 6 p.m. to play games or whatever else some coach has in mind? The NFL thinks so. So does NASCAR, NBA and Major League Baseball. Even ESPN 2 doesn't start bowling until 1 o'clock.

So the soccer gods took over Sunday mornings and no one around here, apparently, thinks this is a bad idea. Except me.

It's more than a game, of course. It means finding the uniform, knee socks, shin guards and the properly sized ball. Filling a water bottle and then driving to the Oklahoma border, parking in another zip code and waking up my daughter in the back seat. Then hiking to find field 23 West.

All the players wear similar uniforms so finding the right team requires binoculars and patience I possess only on Saturdays. Then you get to participate in the world's largest wind tunnel while you watch some guy in knee socks point a yellow flag various directions.

I Googled this pet peeve of mine and found some cities have passed a law to prohibit Sunday morning games. I really don't think that's necessary. However, I would like a law that requires games played that I can watch from the parking lot.

Some people object to Sunday games period. Brigham Young University won't play any games on Sunday. The NCAA forgot about this in 2003 when they put BYU on a tournament track where they would play a Sunday game if they advanced past the second round. It was a huge P.R. disaster even by NCAA standards.

Sometimes famous athletes have declined to play on other days of religious significance. That's what L.A. Dodger pitcher Sandy Koufax did in 1965, when the opening game of the World Series fell on the same day as a major Jewish holiday. Back then, Koufax was a superstar without peer. He was 26-8 in 1965 and had pitched a perfect game just one month earlier.

No matter. He sat it out. The Dodgers lost the first game badly but won the series. The MVP? Koufax.

Any questions?

So the next time it's a Sunday morning and I'm driving halfway to Tulsa with my daughter for a soccer game, I will look to the heavens and wait for a soda bottle to fall from the skies.

When it drops, it will probably hit my car.

Published April, 2006.

High school football games quite the spectacle

I took two of my sons to a high school football game a week ago. St. Thomas Aquinas played Bishop Miege.

There is really nothing quite like high school football games in our culture. They have inspired countless Hollywood movies, including the latest, "Friday Night Lights." The games are one of those rare occasions where father, son and daughter—no matter the age—can enjoy themselves at the same event.

For the adults, the sheer simplicity was refreshing: a game without television timeouts, replay challenges and a 40-minute halftime. The only music was the Aquinas band, not a Guns N' Roses riff played at every kickoff. Football is able to survive—indeed flourish—without ads for the Coors Light twins blaring across a JumboTron. No one is guzzling beer number 56 and then playing target practice in the men's room. No one knows—or even cares—about the head coach's name and certainly has no interest screaming just how stupid they think he is. A ten dollar bill can feed the entire family and goes to fund a field trip for the dance team.

For the students, on the other hand, the entertainment was nowhere near the field. Indeed, for most of the students there, the game was least relevant. My sons ditched me in the stands seconds after arriving. This was a group date for hundreds of teenagers. They gathered behind the bleachers and what went on there defied adult understanding. It was equal parts testosterone and progesterone. And like any good writer, I made mental notes.

As best I could tell, 95 percent of the young women were ready for a casting call to a new movie: "Britney Spears—Attack of the Clones." Clearly these students did not attend either Miege or Aquinas but were bused in from some far away city where their parents were either blind, naïve or both. Shirts were too high, pants too low, with lots of territory in between. Wardrobe malfunctions were imminent.

To further complicate matters, eighth-grade girls appeared to be freshman, sophomores appeared to be seniors, and seniors were halfway through college. The boys could care less. They were too busy finding dates to the upcoming dances, getting instant messaging addresses, working the cell phones and avoiding all parental contact whatsoever.

To complete my fact-finding, on the way home I engaged my sons in a brief Q&A—always a challenge in our household.
"Did you see anyone from your school?"
"I guess."
"Make any new friends?"
"I don't know."
"Will you give your mom a hug when we get inside?"
"Maybe."
Twenty minutes later as we pulled in the driveway, they perked up:
"Is there a home game next week?"
I paused.
"I guess."
"Can we go?"
"I don't know."
"Will you take us?"
"Maybe."
So in my book, high school football games offer something for everyone. Passes, fumbles and penalties. On and off the field.

Published September 2004

I'm a College football guy

Two weeks ago I took my son and a couple of his friends to a KU football game. It was homecoming—KU was playing Texas A&M.

As I took it all in, it became clear to me that football fans fall into two camps. You have the college fans, and then the pro fans. I'm a college guy. And in that contest, it's not even close. Let me count the ways.

College games are still pretty cheap. Pro games are not. College games require less than a full day, and that day, thankfully, is not Sunday.

At college games, you connect with people you haven't seen in 20 years. At Chiefs games, you mingle with fans for whom a 20-year reunion would be too soon. At KU's Memorial Stadium they throw Hail Marys. At Arrowhead they drink Bloody Marys. And margaritas, gin and tonics and 45-ounce beers. The Arrowhead upper deck is not and never will be mistaken for an AA meeting. Where no parent with a brain would ever take their grade-school son or daughter, unless they are hearing-impaired.

There are other contrasts. At KU the cheerleaders are 19 and hope to be doctors. At Arrowhead they are 29 and hope to marry a doctor. Or a linebacker. College games have marching bands, and at some colleges, band members have more prestige than jocks. Take Ohio State, for example. They won the national title in 2003, beating Miami in two overtimes. It was the first national title for Ohio State in 32 years. When the head coach, Jim Tressel, took the microphone, with the nation watching, whom did he thank? He credited "the best damn band in the land." Can you imagine a pro football coach winning the Super Bowl and thanking a band? When that day arrives, look to the heavens. Pigs are flying.

Arrowhead used to have marching bands at halftime. That was back when they went to AFC title games. There are other differences. At Arrowhead, parking in the Gold Reserved section costs you $32.50; for that privilege, you earn a hiking merit badge. New parking assessments are coming, which will be reserved exclusively for those of us in Kansas. In Lawrence, 10 bucks gets you a spot in a front yard directly across from the stadium.

Both have cameras that highlight fans for the big screen. At KU it might be a toddler hugging Baby Jay. At Arrowhead, it's Belly Boy. At KU, post-game, you head to the Wheel. At Arrowhead, post-game, you grip the wheel.

At KU you sit on a hill for pre-game and watch teenagers throw around a football. At Arrowhead you sit on a hill, too. Section 328, row ZZ. At many KU home games you can crash the field and mob the players. Try that at Arrowhead and you'll get Tazered, followed by a tour of the Jackson County jail. Last year KU beat Nebraska, for the first time in 36 years. The fans tore down the goal post and carried it to Potter Lake. Four of those fans were named Keenan. It was, without question, a Top 10 day. The next day Chiefs played someone, somewhere. And lost. Who remembers?

But there is so much more. From the top of Memorial Stadium you can see the Spencer Art Museum, the Campanile and Potter Lake nestled among fall foliage.

Atop Arrowhead you see I-70, Blue Ridge Cut-Off, three gas stations and miles of pavement.

The coaches could not be more different. Herm Edwards is trim. Mark Mangino is not. Edwards wears clothes with labels that read Armani. Mangino's pants say "Coleman." Edwards cries. Mangino sweats. Chiefs fans would add that their team won a Super Bowl in 1970. The Jayhawks have never won a national title. They have beaten Missouri, however, for three years in a row. To most of us, that's a lot more important than the Lombardi trophy.

Published October 21, 2006

Dick Vermeil: My kind of real man

Dick Vermeil owns this town. The media love him. His players love him. The NFL loves him. Chiefs fans would walk over hot coals for the man. And why not? He's been married to the same woman for over 35 years, has 11 grandchildren, is loyal to everyone around him and wears a Super Bowl ring. He also had the good sense to leave St. Louis, where he never attended any of their high schools. And his team is undefeated, of course.

Among the ranks of NFL coaches, Dick Vermeil is one rare bird. Why? He's an emotional teddy bear. He gets weepy in some of the most public forums imaginable—in front of 40 microphones, on live television. Chiefs fans know this and more. They know that when listening on the radio to his postgame news conference and the audio goes silent, to simply be patient. Dick's gone teary again. And about five seconds later, he gets it together and starts hugging everyone around him.

This is the same man who, just hours before, is depicting the toughest of all role models: Extolling his players to blitz, hit and crush the opponent. He coaches a sport that is the epitome of physical strength and endurance. Athletes and coaches must perform under pressure and not choke during the big play. Emotion has always been equated with weakness. Maybe this explains why some coaches cry only when they lose. Roy Williams bawled every time KU lost to a patsy in an early round game in the NCAA tournament—in other words, he cried a lot.

In contrast, Vermeil's predecessor Gunther Cunningham never cried. He left that to the fans. His teams were horrible. Some of his players, thugs. Other NFL coaches would never, ever, be seen holding a tissue. Tampa Bay coach John Gruden, the coach of the defending Super Bowl champ, is nicknamed "Chucky"—named for the demon-possessed doll whose movies featured him chopping up children into tiny pieces. Vermeil's replacement in St. Louis, Mike Martz, is devoid of any emotion whatsoever. Maybe that explains why his team stinks.

Students of history know that several famous leaders were finished at the moment they showed emotion. In 1972, for example, Edmund Muskie was a lock to be the Democratic nominee for president. But the Manchester Union Leader published negative articles about him, including something derogatory about his wife. Muskie broke down and cried. And he promptly became a footnote in political history.

My dad, like most Cold War parents, rarely shows emotion. He's old school. But I'm new school. I make Coach Vermeil look like Darth Vader. I admit it. The first time I cried in public was in the early '70s at my grade school. They showed "Brian's Song" to my class, a movie about Chicago Bears star Brian Piccolo and his terminal cancer diagnosis. I'm not sure what the academic purpose was—maybe because my teacher was a huge KU fan and it featured Gale Sayers. I remember our principal—the meanest nun on the planet—teared up, too.
So Coach Vermeil is single-handedly redefining the image of a real man. Emotion is a good thing, an essential thing, a winning thing.

So add my name to his fan club. And if this team keeps winning all the way to the Super Bowl, somebody better make a run to Costco. Because between Dick and me, there's going to be a run on Kleenex not seen since Brian Piccolo bought the farm.

Published November, 2003

High School basketball: Shawnee Mission East vs. Rockhurst: One for the books.

Movie critics consider "Hoosiers" to be among the top 10 sports movies ever made. I witnessed first-hand the real Kansas version of that movie a week ago Friday, when Shawnee Mission East hosted Rockhurst High School. It was the first high school basketball game I've seen in probably 20 years. And it's clear I've been missing something special.

All of this began to unfold mid-week. Two of our sons attend Rockhurst, but my wife attended East. Her Bunko (aka "Drunko") meetings are a mini-reunion of sorts, class of 1979. Her friends still live in Prairie Village and most have sons and daughters who attend East. One of those friends encouraged us to come, saying, "This game is quite a rivalry."

"Why is that?" I asked.

"I'm not sure," he said. "It's Rockhurst. You know. Public vs. private, Kansas vs. Missouri." He paused for a moment. "Mission Hills vs. Armour Hills, the Lancers vs. Hawklets."

I interrupted him. "What's a Lancer?"

"A Lancer is the East mascot. It's like a Knight but more important. It dates back to the days of Sir Lancelot when Lancers were…." He went on for another minute or two. I stopped him. "OK. I get it. We're coming."

So on Friday night, once inside the gym, a couple things struck me right away. High school gyms are small; maybe the more fitting term is "intimate." Every seat is courtside and none cost more than a buck or two. The action is virtually in your lap. And it's all good.

An hour before the varsity game, the JV game was in full swing, and at the end of regulation it was tied, 50-50. East won in OT and you'd think they just won the state title. On came the varsity. Metro Sports, the cable sports show, went live. The band was playing, the cheerleaders were hopping, and no one moved for four quarters. In my years, I've been to three Final Fours. It would be only a modest exaggeration to say this game packed almost as much excitement. The ticket sales reflected as much: The game sold out two hours before tip-off. Excluded students pressed their faces against the exterior glass and worked their cell phones nonstop, to no avail.

The East students wore powder blue T-shirts. The Rockhurst students wore coats and ties. The grunge/Goth look, I'm happy to report, is history. The varsity game was two hours of solid entertainment without an endless barrage of advertisements or television timeouts. There were other highlights. Like the East dance team. At halftime they "entertained" the students. They came out and did something on the floor. I'm not sure what it was. A dance routine, to be sure. I know it accelerated the breathing patterns of the assembled boys. The Rockhurst students promptly loosened their ties and removed their coats.

The noisemaker of choice was old school—a cow bell. So was the program—one page, typed on what appeared to be a 1972 IBM typewriter. It contained all the information you needed, and was, of course, free. Popcorn was 50 cents.

There were other traditions you won't find at a college or NBA game. Before the start of the game, four women in uniform holding trumpets walked to half-court, and then they criss-crossed while the East students stood in reverence. "Those are the Heralders," my wife told me. I nodded as if I understood.
At the end of the third quarter the announcer introduced the East Kansas 5A state debate champions. The place went crazy. Again, I wondered to myself: "Who are they introducing at the next home game … a couple Nobel Prize winners?"

East poured it on the Hawklets—which was a major upset—and the East AD admonished the students "please don't rush the court—let the players and coaches shake hands." I smiled and said to myself "sure." The last time I heard something like this was KU/Nebraska football, when the announcer warned the students to stay clear of the goal posts. By the time he finished his sentence, the uprights were getting dropped in Potters Lake. Here, to my shock, the students obliged.

And as the Keenans left the gym, the band was playing a song, the final words of which were "God watch over SME." Prayer answered.

SME 54, Rockhurst 45.

Published February 4, 2006

6

Odds and Ends

Sometimes my columns don't fall into any particular category. These are some of my favorites.

Class reunions offer chance to visit the past

I just returned from my high school reunion. Reunions have no peer in our culture. They are like dysfunctional family gatherings held at a singles bar.

In some places, like St. Louis, class reunions are the most important social event of the entire year. They go on for days—with formal dinners, family picnics, cake walks and the like.

My high school class isn't in those leagues. We had our five-year reunion in a wheat field. It was an old-fashioned kegger. That's what we did in western Kansas back then. One of my classmates brought his twin pit bull terriers, Bartles and James. That's the truth.

But this latest reunion was no ordinary one. It was our 25th. It's code for your age, of course. So yes, I'm old. Deal with it.

Previous reunions taught me that such events are best enjoyed without your spouse. It saves you from awkward introductions to old girlfriends and the subsequent interrogations that follow.

Here are a couple other things I've learned.

•When a complete stranger approaches, gives you a hug and kiss, and asks "Remember me," say the magic words: "You haven't changed one bit."

•And when your class's version of Al Bundy (read: former star athlete) seeks a high five, reassure him, again, that yes, in fact, he was the greatest jock on the planet.

This reunion played out like the others. In one corner, various married couples clung to each other tightly. Typically, they were enjoying nuptials for the second or third time. Another group was the singles. They were dolled up and ready for action. The women sported plunging necklines and typically had new teeth and tans. The men, well, there's only so much one can do.

Initially, you could cut the tension with a butter knife. Someone forgot name tags, and that created a strange kind of guessing game. Everyone stared at everyone else, and you could read at least one thing on their faces: "Am I as old as you look?"

Ninety-nine percent of every conversation was about children or, in some cases, grandchildren. How many. How old. Many came prepared with photographs. Some had glamour shots. I had none. I was too busy trying to remember times before children. When my life was simple, fun and really cheap.

During the course of the evening, my buddies and I concluded that 1977 was a great year. One worthy of a great class. It had the finest movies ("Smokey and the Bandit") the finest music (Eagles' "Hotel California" and Fleetwood Mac's "Rumours") and the finest prom ever held at a Holiday Inn. It was Fast Times meet The Breakfast Club.

The next morning, my dad reminded me of some things I had forgotten. The class of 1977 had a football team that went 0-10 (By season's end, they held pep rallies in a phone booth). No graduates played college sports. We had no National Merit scholars, academic All-Americans or Rhodes scholars. On graduation night, it was the high school's faculty that celebrated the most.
Details, I replied.

The next day I returned home to Johnson County. The driveway was strewn with in-line skates, scooters, abandoned Super Soakers and busted water balloons. The mail included a sizable bill for my son's new braces. My wife promptly handed me the baseball schedule for the next two days and spun me around with instructions to find my son's mouth guard somewhere in the back seat of the car.

At that moment, I clearly understood the wisdom of an extended class reunion.

Published July 2002

Raking Leaves: Let Nature Run its course

The election is finally over. So now we can discuss more important things, like leaf raking. Hardly anyone really "rakes" leaves anymore. Sometime in the mid-'80s, homeowners replaced rakes with electric- or gas-powered devices designed to attack and destroy leaves. It seems everyone has one, except me.

I'll never get one either. As I see it, when leaves fall they should be left alone to follow whatever pathway nature takes them, which is hopefully just across the property line. If leaves are beautiful while clinging to a branch, they are just as special when lying on the ground, particularly when it's windy.

So last weekend while on a walk with the dog, I took an informal survey of the popular yard tools around the county. This is what I found:

• **Blower/sucker.** This weaponry is a status symbol on par with a Hummer or Viper in the driveway. Once equipped, these owners strut around the yard like a peacock in heat. These machines can either suck or blow at the flip of a switch. Some even mulch the leaves once sucked. The advertising brochure for one boasts of a "rounded wind tunnel design" that enhances performance.

They come with shoulder straps and seat belts so you can stay in one place when you inhale half the county. These suckers can even inhale leaves still dangling from the tree. They have names like "Vac N Mulch," "Leaf Hog," "Leaf Eliminator" and "Leaf B Gone." A neighbor told me that his sucker can dispose of wasp nests, crabgrass and even unwanted pets. Just plant your feet firmly, aim, fire and debag.

• **Blower.** The air goes just one way. These contraptions were cool 10 years ago but became less popular when their owners went deaf from the noise. Some are so loud they are banned in California. No kidding. One neighbor gave me the scoop on these. He told me, through sign language, that these are great for blow drying your wife's hair when she is two hours late for the office party.

One blower I checked out on the Internet had a maximum air velocity—honestly now—of 200 mph. This one came with a double shoulder harness, hip pad and anti-vibration handle. If the poor sap is not properly strapped in when he fires it up, he gets a free trip into the next subdivision.

Anything this powerful has countless uses. Blowing all your leaves across the street is just the beginning. Other uses: sanitizing your teenagers' socks and shoes; flying a kite on a windless day; greeting your mother in law when she pulls into the driveway, exposing your neighbor's toupee.

• **Lawn mowers.** These days, mowers come with a huge bag that compresses tons of leaves in one Sunday drive. On very rare occasions you see Johnson County residents using the old fashioned push lawn mowers to mow leaves. I wasn't even aware they even sold those anymore. It's like driving a Yugo in a parade of Mercedes. In Hallbrook, it'll get you a citation from the homes association.

• **Rakes.** Old timers still like rakes, but they are essential accessories. These are the yellow "Claws of Life" that are like cymbals for your hands. It helps grab lots of leaves while your neighbor's blower is adding to your leaf collection.
EBay sells this thing called the "Ultimate Mulcher" to grind everything into microscopic sized particles. That's the last thing my house needs. I can see my sons "testing it out" with trees, large shrubs, school uniforms, grade cards, Beanie Babies. I can hear it now: "Hey, Dad, guess what this used to be?"

My wife wants me to get a blower/sucker. She knows this is basically cheap therapy, that spending the afternoon abusing helpless leaves builds self-esteem for the JoCo henpecked husbands. What she doesn't know is that I get my therapy already—disguised in this column.

Published November 2004.

Getting the annual physical

Our country has great health care, but that does little to make men feel good about getting an annual checkup.

I can't explain it, but women—more accurately, mothers—seem far more in tune with their health. And their doctors. Moms love their children's doctors, too. My wife places more trust in our pediatrician than anyone else on the planet. If a pediatrician ever ran for president, it would be a victory margin that would put Saddam Hussein to shame.

So, all of this emotional baggage comes crashing down on me when it's time for my annual physical. Let me be clear: I like my doctor. To begin with, he's on my insurance plan. He's also roughly my age, and that means his body is falling apart, just like mine. He's very busy, so other people must like him, too. And I relish the comfort of knowing he has the confidence of others.

You're leery, after all, of the handyman who bids to do work on your house and has time available for the next two years.

My previous doctor, however, was too popular. And all his patients seemed to get sick on the day of my physical. His office had bulletproof glass separating the staff from the unhealthy world. If you were deemed worthy of addressing, the nurse pulled the glass back and sneered at you. One day, I decided that entrusting your life to someone who treated you as livestock was a bad thing, so I found a new doctor.

On the anointed day, I arrived at the doctor's office with my insurance card in hand. The room was full, and they were running behind. I stared at everyone else waiting and speculated about which of their body parts weren't functioning properly. People who arrived after me got called in before me. I waited. And waited. While I did, I read copies of Woman's Day and Good Housekeeping.

Eventually, it was my turn. Someone took me to the holding cell and left me there. I think those rooms have one-way mirrors so nurses can giggle at nervous patients. The examining table—probably used as an altar for some kind of religious sacrifice on weekends—was covered with paper they threw in the "biohazard" container after I left.

I knew that something quite unnatural was about to happen there. With my body. And my heart was racing.

The nurse arrived. My heart picked up the pace. So what did she do? Measure my blood pressure, of course. She left. More waiting. And then it happened. The doctor arrived, holding a folder that contained all my medical secrets. He broke the ice by talking about "guy topics" like sports and then awkwardly transitioned to bodily functions. What works, what doesn't. After the short Q&A, he started the exam. Ears, eyes, nose, elsewhere. The easy stuff. Then, it got complicated. Because this is a "family newspaper," just let me say that I'm not sure what the prostate is, but it's obviously very hard to locate.

Once the doctor was done, he asked me if I had any questions. I tried to remember all the times over the past year my wife told me to "Ask your doctor about that. But I could only manage to stare at him like a second-grader freezing in his first confession. "No, nothing." And it was over. Just like that.

Someday, a doctor will figure out that making men feel comfortable is good business. When that day arrives, the waiting room will be a sports bar, and the magazines will be Power Tool Illustrated. The nurses will be grandmotherly and wear those cute little white caps they wore on Marcus Welby. Appointments will start and finish on time. Blood pressures will be checked at the end—not the beginning—of the exam.

And men's health will never be the same again.

Published October, 2003

Whatever Happened to Customer Service?

A couple years ago companies began firing employees that I used to find very helpful. Customer service departments no longer have service or customers.

Wal-Mart joined the computer age by installing what they call "self-checkout" lanes. That's a euphemism for "you do our work." These lanes are popular with the truly brain-dead customers, who look for a scanner code on things like watermelons and food samples while half the store waits behind them. Gas stations got in the act, and went from full service to no service overnight.

So where did these people go? Some went to the Lake of the Ozarks, where they climbed in a boat, got drunk and ran over waterskiers. Some went to Chiefs training camp. But that doesn't account for everyone. And then suddenly this mystery was solved. I learned three weeks ago where everyone else was to be found—at a cell phone store in Overland Park.

And on the day that I joined half the world's population, I was in a really bad mood. Anytime I waste time with a cell phone I get grumpy. When the cell phone belongs to my teenage son, my mood gets worse.

As I drove to the store, it occurred to me that absolutely nothing about today's cell phone business is simple. Or convenient. Take the cell phone bill, for instance. Mine weighs 10 pounds. My last bill was 58 pages with size four font. No kidding.

Four phones, one calling plan I can never begin to decipher. The Da Vinci code plot is more straightforward. There are service charges, usage charges, surcharges, taxes, and fees. Peak, off-peak, non-peak, twins peak. My kids care about none of these details, of course, unless their phone suddenly stops ringing.

And that day was here. And since I can't trust my sons to make any decisions regarding their phones, this was a task that only I could handle.

So anyway, back to the store. This place has high-tech things—phones with cameras, laptops, flat-panel screens. But it lacked something low tech—service. Inside the door a woman greeted me. So far so good, I said to myself. She took my name, and handed me a piece of paper back.

Like a Hallmark card to make you feel special. So I waited for a couple minutes and sales guy No. 1 called my name. He was young, very young, but pleasant. I explained that my son's phone didn't work, that it could be because of a billion reasons, but that I did not want to buy a new one if I could avoid it. He took the phone, said the specialists would evaluate it, and I should return in an hour. I had "a reservation." Like a restaurant.

When I returned, I waited. That's then I met sales guy No. 2. This sales guy was older than number one—a lot older, maybe 17 or 18. And this is when I learned about "the door." It's the door that leads into a room where the employees have to enter and exit every 30 seconds. I have no idea what's behind the door. Maybe the Wizard of Oz, Yoda, Jabba the Hut, my mother-in-law.

This magical door was similar to the door at Dick's Sporting Goods shoe department. Where the shoe salesman disappears to find my son's shoe size. 13DDD. On this day, the sales guy and Yoda were in an intense discussion.

There was trouble, I could smell it. My blood pressure was peaking. Phone broken, remanufactured model had issues, unpaid bill, who knows. When he left me the third time, I noticed that another employee had moved very close to where I was standing—the security guard. He was pretending not to watch me. He studiously avoided eye contact. Something he learned at the Barney Fife school of cell phone store security.

I decided that if he spoke to me, my reply was very predictable: "Are you talking to me?"

Never happened, fortunately. Sales guy No. 2 emerged with a remanufactured phone; I declined all the service plans, contract options, wrote him a check, and headed to a place more comfortable than this store—my hot car.

Published October 2006.

Editorial comment: The following column generated the most e-mails of any column I have written. It also spurred three letters to the Editor, all in support of this column, which was written after a week of flat out wrong television weather forecasts.

Forecasters deserve special treatment for goofs

The first thing we do," said a character in Shakespeare's "Henry VI, Part 2," "let's kill all the lawyers." I have a much better idea. Let's start by banishing the weather forecasters. And when we are finished with them, we will go after Janet Jackson, her brother Michael and any other occupants at the Neverland Ranch. Then we will move to everyone involved at MTV. Our lives will improve substantially.

Weather forecasters are on everyone's hit list, and no wonder. These talking heads come from the General Custer school of leadership. They take clueless to an art form. I'd take Punxsutawney Phil over any of them. Plus he has better looking hair, makes a forecast once a year, and then disappears for the rest of the year. We should be so lucky.

Like all of us, I have no tolerance for the weather forecasters. They employ the finest computer models, latest technology, and nonstop promotions to be consistently wrong on every account. They begin identifying the storm when it's hovering near Hawaii. It then moves toward us for about a month, all the while they hype its potential, with snow forecasts that range from inches to feet. To fill time as it approaches, they show us time-lapse photos of the sunset and sunrise, and give us the record highs and lows over the last 100 years. They have "live shots" from various locations in Raymore and Kearney. Who cares?

Within 72 hours of the storm, they go into "sweeps mode." They replace regular programming with "storm alert" shows, all to cover a non-event that moves about 20 miles per hour. The storm alert promos include dramatic audios and graphics. Military invasions have less hype. They tease the viewers nonstop, with empty promises: "Coming up, the latest forecast," which they don't actually show until you sit through another 20 minutes of commercials.

This past Sunday, in the eight hours of special "live" programming, they first canceled the only intelligent news programming of the entire week. Then they needed some filler. So they sent various reporters out "live" to walk the streets and sidewalks to tell us what we already knew: There was no snow and really not much ice either.

Meanwhile, Chip the reporter kept admonishing viewers to avoid doing exactly what he was doing: wasting time outside with no real purpose. And then you had Biff live from the salt mines. "I'm here live and they have lots of salt! Back to you!" Never in the history of local television has more been made of less.

And then the mother lode arrived on Thursday. We went from a slight "dusting" to a true snowstorm. If they spent less time in makeup counters and more time calling people in places like Goodland, we might get more value.

After all, the last time I checked, most storms come from the west, and there isn't much separating Kansas City from Denver. It's pretty flat, and there's not much water. How complicated can it be, really? The FCC should require these stations should add another label to their existing slogans of "live, local, investigative and wrong!"

So with the real storm comes real cancellations, which means that parents who can't navigate the streets in snow promptly climb in their cars to drop off their children off at various locations throughout the city.

If I were king for a day, I would be a weather forecaster. My report would go something like this: "It's February, and that means it's going to be cold, probably below freezing. If it snows, you will see it on your lawn tomorrow. How much it snows depends on how much falls from the sky. You should not believe anyone who forecasts an amount. Tonight at 10 I will tell you how much snow we received. I will do so in the studio and not from a helicopter, on top of a building, and certainly not standing in the middle of the interstate. I will be live and local but won't insult your intelligence by reminding you of that the entire broadcast. Whatever food you have in your pantry and refrigerator will get you through the next 12 hours. If you want to know what the roads are like, call your relatives in Topeka."

The entire report will take 30 seconds.

How refreshing.

Published February 2004

'Bachelor' viewing: Sign of no life

For network television, this is sweeps week. That means all the networks are rolling out their best shows. And though this is not the TV section, and I'm no TV critic, I have some credentials on this. You see, my wife is addicted to one television show—the same one that has hooked many of the housewives in North America: "The Bachelor." If none of this sounds familiar to you, you either have no wife or no TV. In which case, you have something I don't have—a life. So permit me to tell you what you are missing.

This series started out with 25 "contestants." They included Tara, April, Jehan, Princess, Shiloh, Liza, and Venus, just to name a few. None, I suspect, were members of Mensa. Over the last month or so they were "whittled down." Which led to last week's episode.

This is what I learned watching it Monday night for the first time. This show is not about a bachelor. It's about a gigolo. The plot lines, well there is no plot, simply tight camera angles where the guy exchanges mindless small talk with one date after another. The women wear virtually no clothes, and what they do wear hangs from a thin strap. They are bronzed, head to toe, except their teeth, which glow in the dark.

Most of the scenes are over some dimly lit dinner, and they whisper as if no one else can hear them, except, of course, for the entire free world.

The bachelor, Travis, is a medical doctor. Which is a good thing. That way he can dispense the free meds his future bride will require when she becomes a footnote in television trivia and turns into a raging lunatic.

This show is filmed in Paris. You would never know it, however, because most of the scenes are in bed or in hot tubs. Ninety-nine percent of this stuff is staged. I suspect this when he says, "Hey, let's go climb a mountain." His date acts surprised but just happens to be wearing a harness and mountain boots.

"The Bachelor" is noteworthy for what's NOT in the show. No church scenes. No kitchen scenes. If Travis had a brain in his head, he would ask each of them for their favorite chocolate-chip cookie recipe. Now that would be true reality TV.

All of this culminates with something they call the Rose Ceremony. My wife sits with her legs up against her chest, clutching the remote. She has clearly decided who the right choice is for Travis, which she then tries to tell him as the camera pans to each of the remaining suitors. "NO, TRAVIS, NOT HER!! SHE IS A PHONY!!" My daughter agrees. "NOT HER—SHE'S MEAN!!"

Last week there were three contestants left. One was from Overland Park, but she got booted. That left Sarah, who is a kindergarten teacher. She loves kids. The other is named Moana (no typo, folks). I'm pretty sure that she is not skilled at instructing 6-year-olds. My wife has noticed that Moana has a tattoo on her posterior.

Guess which one my wife thinks HAS GOT TO GO!!!!

The part I like is when the bachelor takes the spurned reject down a hallway for a "farewell hug." The rebuked loser always cries, and says the words "hurt" and "feel" 20 times. The bachelor says, "I'm sorry" and "mistake" 25 times. Kleenex stock soars.

Next week, my wife and daughter will be watching. I probably will too. Go Sarah.

Published April, 2006.

It's a party! Bring your wallet!

Small business drives our economy. And the hottest businesses right now are in your subdivision, maybe in your living room. These are the "home shopping"/ direct selling businesses. They have no overhead, no employees, no inventory but a sizable bank account. And with the arrival of the holidays, it's time for eggnog, Christmas cookies and a Longaberger basket party.

These sales parties are hot. Really hot. Every soccer mom has either attended one or will shortly. It's bunko meets Amway where the booze flows freely and the wallets open quickly. It's like Mary Kay, but no pink Cadillac. It's Hobby Lobby without plastic flowers. It's Toys R Us without an army of children sneezing on you. When you host a party, you get free gifts. When you convince a friend to host a party, you get valuable merchandise. When you convince all your friends to host lots of parties, you move to Mission Hills.

The success of all this is entirely dependent on creating a "husband-free zone," which means the distinction between wants and needs is tossed to the wind like a tattered credit card receipt. The drill goes like this. One of my wife's friends invites as many people as possible to her home. My wife feels obligated.

"She wants me to come by. I won't buy anything." A familiar line. The women gather, mingle, gossip. Items are on display. The cheapest item is $75. The host then breaks out the mimosas, then margaritas, then Captain Morgan. My wife's purse becomes suddenly lighter. Two hours later we have enough Pampered Chef accessories for a room addition.

This craze is now into candles, spices, kids clothes, toys, jewelry, scrapbooks, picture frames, plants, baby clothes, lingerie, beauty care products. The hottest thing right now is the "Bag Daddy," where women host parties to design their own handbags. At these shindigs, you make a new purse but have then have no money left to carry in it. According to USA Today, the home-selling scene is a $28 billion business. Forget Tupperware. No one would dare leave these parties with anything made of plastic.

Which brings me to the Longabergers. I can only assume this is named for an entrepreneur who is a neighbor to Bill Gates. For the uninformed, these are baskets that have reached collector status. Once you own a basket, you need to own countless other "essentials," like basket liners, for example. These have replaced the Beanie Baby as the "gotta have" item of the year. They have little functional purpose and less intrinsic value. But that does not make them cheap. Hardly.

My wife has never hosted one of these things, but for her friends who have, she has financed elaborate family vacations and countless SUV upgrades. So as I researched this craze, some things started to interest me, like the word billion.

So, I'm pleased to announce that my wife will be hosting a special event. Wives and mothers across the county are invited. For the afternoon that we will meet, husbands should go play golf. This will be an interactive gathering with prize drawings for rare collectibles. When you arrive at our show, sales consultants will direct you to a table of show items—the finest Ginsu kitchen accessories available today.

To call them knives would insult the ancient Inca tribes that first forged them over an open fire. These are limited edition, rare, collectible carving tools. Available for a limited time. All highly functional and extremely decorative. They will transform your kitchen overnight into a world-class entertaining dining facility. As for the date, and location, that will have to wait until the conclusion of the Chiefs season. A party this big requires Arrowhead Stadium.

Published December, 2003

7

My Dad the Lawyer

For the last two years I have published a monthly column in the Kansas Bar Journal. Here are four of my favorites.

LARRY E.

KEENAN

FOR

COUNTY ATTORNEY

BARTON COUNTY

Qualified through Experience

Every eight year old boy adores his father. That's no real revelation, obviously. But when the father's profession is being a lawyer in a small town, it adds another dimension to the equation. And when your dad is one of a handful attorneys in the entire county, then his level of importance gets bumped up even more. And if he happens to be the former County Attorney, he is on a par with the Police Chief, the County Sheriff, and the parish priest. And in 1967, in Great Bend, no one was more beholden to one Larry Keenan than me. Followed only by my kid brother Marty and my older brother Tim.

As most readers know, in the late 60s, lawyers were the stuff of Atticus Finch, Perry Mason, and Clarence Darrow. "My Cousin Vinnie" was nowhere on the horizon. This was a profession whose role models exemplified true giants in our times. No surprise, then, that many young boys wanted to be a lawyer first and a doctor second. But what made it even more appealing was my dad's law partner was his best friend and mentor: his older brother, Robert. That was a one-two family punch that no other professional could come close to matching. As an added bonus they had their own office building with the name across the top: "Keenan & Keenan." It was cool, really cool.

But what made all this adoration a bit unusual was that neither I nor my brothers had any real clue what our Dad did on a daily basis. Dad took client confidentiality to an art form. Sure we watched Perry Mason every day, but Dad had no Della Street or Paul Drake on his payroll. While he did possess a law enforcement badge—which he laid prominently on his dresser—there was very little crime in Barton County, and as best I recall, there were few high profile trials. Yet this added to the mystery of his ways. There was a huge separation between his world and ours. And that's the way he wanted it.

On the rare days we were allowed to visit his office, we stared at the Xerox machine like a caveman watching fire for the first time. We hoarded the legal pads, rubber bands and sugar cubes from the break room. It was Joyland meets Office Depot. In the back of the office he had a huge black safe. Taped on the front was the sign: "this safe contains no money or other valuables. Only wills and trusts." That disclaimer was more than preposterous. It was laughable, Keystone Cops stupidity. We knew that the safe contained the Hope diamond, a bloody knife and pistol used in a murder that had not hit the newsstand. This safe contained all the secrets, which is why we tried to crack it, using the time tested techniques we had seen on Mission Impossible. This occupied us for hours at a time, which precisely served dad's purpose.

But there was a rare occasion when Dad's world intersected with ours. And when it did, it was a gift from the gods. That happened when a client needed to see Dad at the house. There was trouble in River City. This was sinner meets saint; someone did something horrible and was pleading for redemption. So Larry would take the client out to the balcony—the only place he could gain some privacy in our home. We would dash for the basement, and open the windows below the balcony. We could hear bits and pieces but never enough to connect the dots.

This drove us crazy, of course, and asking Larry for the secrets would only give away our rudimentary technique. But then one day all that changed. My dad gained a new client. This man had a penchant for two things: excessive alcohol consumption, and late night phone calls to his attorney. And when he dabbled in the former, he always did the latter. And for some strange reason, he always called when my parents were "out for dinner."—typically the Great Bend Petroleum club (that's where every professional went in those days).

And when the phone rang around midnight, we did not need caller ID. "Is Larry there?" Those three words required about 30 seconds for full delivery. "I'm sorry, Larry isn't home. May I take a message?" The man's reply was identical, every time. It was an expression that started with "bull" and ends with a word that rhymes with hit. The first word he repeated a couple times. The second word he needed to say only once. The written word cannot do it justice, of course. But the fact that Dad had a client who drank, and even worse, cussed, fit perfectly into our wildest notions of his law practice.

So eventually my brothers and I quenched our thirst for information. We got the full story on father's law practice. And nothing we learned diminished our admiration for his work, his clients, or the profession we all share. Perhaps that explains why today my two brothers Marty and Tim practice law with one Larry Keenan. And his brother Robert.

Published March 2005.

We knew the real killer before the first commercial break

In case you haven't noticed, lawyer shows are the rage these days. "Law & Order" and "Boston Legal" are just two of them. I suspect most lawyers have little interest in fictional accounts of our profession. But many of my nonlawyer friends watch these shows. So I watched one. It was "Boston Legal"—whose senior partner is William Shatner, who went from Captain Kirk to the lead partner in a Boston law firm. The episode was the most preposterous thing I have ever seen. It was fiction beyond a screenwriter's wildest dreams. Shatner was more believable when he wore a polyester jump suit and barked out commands to Sulu.

You see, I'm an expert on Hollywood and the law. I grew up watching "Perry Mason." In 1972 in Barton County, our home got two television channels, both beamed in from Wichita. Based on the signal strength, Mars seemed closer. And on channel 12, the afternoon show was "Perry Mason." In one hour you had a murder, an arrest, Mason retained, witnesses interviewed, alibis developed, and then the courtroom scene. Perry Mason was our star. It was real TV, real lawyering. For some reason the programming guy at KAKE 12 thought that 10-year-old kids would watch this stuff over cartoons. And we did. In spades.

Back then the practice of law was simple. Perry had no use for the billable hour. No retainer. Justice was in demand and Mason was happy to deliver. My two brothers and I sat and watched every episode. The stock in trade for most episodes was blackmail schemes with embarrassing photos. Like a man caught with his shirt off or something else incredibly benign by today's standards. The shows had great titles, which Google helped me find: "The Case of the Lazy Lover," "The Case of the Screaming Woman," "The Case of the Fatal Fortune," and "The Case of the Runaway Corpse." In contrast, "Boston Legal" has shows titled "Breast in Show" (aired in February).

Perry's success was due to his crack team, Della Street and Paul Drake. Della was so much more than just a secretary. She was a know-it-all without being a know-it-all. Paul Drake was like her male clone. He was part detective, part paralegal, and all dedication. He knew everyone and everything. In almost every plot Perry would hit some dead end, and things would look bleak. That's when Paul would say something like "I have a bartender friend downtown who knows something about handgun ballistics. I'll go pay him a visit." Five minutes later, he would return with a gleam in his eye. He broke the case but couldn't say anything until after the commercial break.

The Internet is brimming with Web pages dedicated to this stuff. I found it interesting that someone has spent hours piecing together dialogue between Paul and Della to prove they were actually having an affair behind Perry's back. I immediately called my brother, Marty, for his reaction. "That's outrageous," he blurted.

"You and I know Della was too dedicated to try any hanky panky. Plus, she adored Perry. That was clear from the outset." I agreed.

Anyway, back to Perry. He was fully capable of acquitting his client and obtaining a confession at the same time. Seconds apart. The suspect was never hiding out on some distant island. There was no "America's Most Wanted" because no one went on the lam. Instead they were in court, awaiting the moment when they spilled their guts. The Fifth Amendment, as far we knew back then, had not been added to the Constitution.

The confession was dramatic. It often involved some jealous love interest. They not only confessed, they went into detail with motive and everything. It was like a "confession in a box." The show would be 45 seconds from concluding. I would sit there and say, "How are they going to wrap this up?" And then it would happen. The camera would go into the assembled courtroom galley. Some woman would start to cry. "He lied to me. He said we would get married, but he lied. He had photos, too. I had no choice. I did it. I shot him in the back. I'm sorry." She would fall to the ground and faint. The camera would fade to Perry, and he would nod as if to say, "I knew it all along."

District Attorney Burger was the embodiment of the team that plays the Harlem Globe Trotters and has never won a basketball game. He deserved an Emmy. When he looked shocked, amazed, and stunned you actually believed him. There were other bit players, like detectives and policemen, but they didn't matter. At the end of the show, there was always a scene where they tied up loose ends and made certain viewers were able to connect all the dots and understand the various plot lines. That was one part of the show we never watched. Such spoon feeding was best left to grade-school kids in places like Derby. We knew the real killer before the first commercial break.

Published April, 2006.

Learning Kansas Geography poses special challenges for my children

I have lived in Johnson County for twenty years. But Barton County is really home—Great Bend to be precise. And as long as my dad and two brothers live and practice law there, that won't change. So I have a close affinity for Western

Kansas. I have learned that most of the people from Kansas City—particularly Johnson County—are, like me, transplants from some other part of the world. This has made one question quite popular—sooner or later, people ask one question: ***where ya from***? 98% of the time this is one of those "filler questions" strangers ask because they already mentioned the weather and the Chiefs' latest loss. And 99% of the time they really don't care about your reply. Until you give it.

At that point, they get the chance to show how smart they really are. They stick their neck out and pretend to spout off some level of sophistication about Kansas geography. To them, it's I-70 with a couple rest stops between here and Limon. They ask "which part?" I make it easy on them. "Central Kansas. Near Salina." As soon as those words roll off my lips, they go blank. Their eyes glaze over. You hear an ocean roar near their ears. To them, Salina sounds like something they ate at the Carlos O'Kelly's condiment bar last night. Their mind eventually returns to this planet and they declare, confidently, "Sure. Near Wichita, right?" To non-natives, Wichita is the most popular guess. "Yeah, that's right." And then I look for the nearest exit, fire alarm or men's restroom.

So no sooner do I bemoan the geographical inadequacies of Eastern Kansans, I encounter the same confusion from my friends from Great Bend. They know central and west and don't know jack about the East. They can't sort Shawnee from Shawnee Mission from Mission to Mission Hills, Westwood from Westwood Hills, Prairie Village from Prairie View. To them, Johnson County is either Overland Park or Olathe.

So all of this confusion has bothered me a bit, in case you couldn't tell. Since I'm one of those sentimental Kansas guys who tears up at the sight of the Kansas flag, I want my four children to break the mold. I want them to know both ends of this great state and be able to intelligently converse with strangers no matter where they are from. So long as it's about Kansas, of course. No one should care about Missouri, obviously. I want them to know that Wichita County does not include Wichita and Johnson County does not include Johnson City. Chase is not in Chase County, and Quivira Lake and Quivira refuge are separated by 270 miles. Hays and Haysville are nowhere close. That Kansas has a fondness for five saints: St. Francis, St. George, St. John, St. Mary's and St. Paul. All fine cities with lots of holy people.

They must understand that you can travel to Columbus, Minneapolis, Nashville, Plains, Pittsburg, Sun City, Tampa, and Syracuse in one day in one car. Where you can visit Zurich, Moscow, and Frankfort, without needing a passport. I want them to remember that my mom grew up in Kingman, and my dad in Seward and that they were married in Wichita. East Wichita, to be exact. December 19, 1952.

So in the course of a couple thousand road trips to see my brothers in Great Bend, my sister in Wichita, or frequent trips to Colorado, I've filled the role as fulltime tour director. I have yelled to them, for example, on Hi-way 150, that Strong City had two world champion rodeo riders in the early 1900's. Along I-70 I tell them that the Garden of Eden is really in Lucas. "Adam and Eve were from Kansas" they marveled. That Hays is where they filmed Paper Moon, circa 1973. That "In Cold Blood" has a scene filmed at the A&W in Great Bend. Never mind that now it's a Chinese restaurant. I tell them that movie starred Robert Blake back when he ***played*** a murder suspect instead of actually ***being one***. Most of the time when I play tour guide I'm lucky to get a grunt in return, if not complete silence, but that does not deter me one bit. I'm making progress.

My dad told me it's better to light one candle than to curse the darkness. He's right. He told me that driving along I-70. I probably grunted in response.

Published February, 2005.

Practicing Law and Golf: Two things that don't mix

This column is dedicated to the annual Bar Convention and playing golf. Two things that really have little in common with each other, except for the annual KBA golf tournament. For most of us, the bar convention is a great time to get together and reconnect with fellow bar members. Earn some CLE, trade war stories, relax. And then someone decides to play golf. And that's when things start to get ugly.

See, I don't think golf mixes well with lawyering. There are exceptions, of course. Bobby Jones was a great golfer, maybe the best ever, then he was a great lawyer, but he never excelled at both at the same time. That was no accident. Golf eats up more time than playing Sudoku. In my opinion, golf is best left to other professions who have a lot of free time on their hands—like banking and insurance salesmen. Golf takes about eight hours to play and when its over you get home to find out why some lawyers hate to do mediate domestic disputes. Been there.

So anyway, back to my story. When I was young and stupid, I used to play golf with strangers. The centerpiece of this was the KBA convention. I figure playing golf with fellow attorneys around the state was a great idea. Until I tried it.

This put into motion a disaster of titanic proportions. It was the Bar Convention, circa 1987. Location: Topeka. Back then my uncle Denny from Great Bend and I paired up. But it takes four to make a team. So we were paired up with two other lawyers whose names I hope to never remember. I'm sure they remember. They can't forget that day, try as they might. When you play with strangers, right away you look for visual clues about their skill level.

Easy things, like the quality of their shoes and shirts, for example. Do their clubs have brand names or knock off names. Is the Nike swoosh forward or backward, for instance. Golf also has certain trappings that some people buy to give them the "look.." Denny and I had no use for this silliness. We resembled two yahoos who flunked the dress code at the Caddy Shack. So the next indication is the tee shot. And that tells your partners whether the next four hours will be a high five convention or a living hell.

The first hole tee box is the one with the largest audience. Spectators stand by and watch with great anticipation. Everyone was standing there when Denny took center stage. He walked up, did all the right things—tossed some blades of grass into the wind, nodded, as if to say "got it" and then took a couple practice swings. I said to myself "This is great. Playing with my uncle." And he started his backswing. He then unleashed a furious swing. It had the aerodynamic fury of a 747. Except I saw no ball. Anywhere. Until I looked at his golf tee. And there it sat. It had not moved. A total and complete whiff.

When someone whiffs in golf, it's a top ten horrible moment. When someone whiffs in golf on the first tee, it moves to number two. And when you whiff on the first tee with total strangers on your foursome, its number one. Its on par with watching someone's pants fall down during an airport security check, someone tripping down the wedding isle; a man's hair piece flying off in a stiff breeze, someone's dental bridge dropping to the plate. When Denny whiffed, life went in slow motion. You could hear crickets chirping on the back nine. Bald Eagles circling over the Artic were audible. The assembled audience pretended they never saw it. They quickly averted their glace to the nearby water tower or closed their eyes completely as if to meditate. I had to watch. He was my partner.

What immediately follows is that no one dares to say a thing. You wait for the whiff-master to acknowledge his folly. Denny paused and stared forward, expecting the ball to land in the fairway. Then he understood the enormity of it all. Golf etiquette says you hit another ball as fast as humanly possible. Which he did. For all intents and purposes, however, the day was done. Our partners knew the next four hours would turn to nine hours. So we obliged. Denny and I started creating divots that would swallow most golf carts. The bevy cart became our constant companion and by the end of the last hole we didn't care one bit about the leader board.

So at this year's KBA convention, when you are looking for that ball in the weeds on the back nine, and your day is pretty bad, think of Uncle Denny. That should brighten your day.

Published May 2006

8

The Holidays

Mixing four toddlers with the religious holidays is truly the best of times and the worst of times.

Christmas decorations and my life: A brief history

Christmas decorations are like my life. They started simple and cheap, and then everything changed. Sort of like the homes you hang them on. Add to the mix children, moving companies and a jumbo mortgage. And then one day your electrical meter spins like a gyroscope and KCPL invites you to its board meetings.

From my perspective, here is a quick historical overview.

The early years. For us, it was early '80s and life was worry free. Our first home was in Fairway. Phone booths come bigger. My wife was gainfully employed. We were DINKS—double income, no kids. I had never met anyone called a pediatrician and cared nothing about things like growth charts. My waist size was 32. My hair was coal black. Life was never better.

Decorations were easy—some lights went around the front door, tossed over two trees in the front yard. I needed a footstool and five minutes. Followed by a cold beer, and then quality time with my newlywed wife.

After our first Christmas, circa 1987, I noticed my wife became proficient at test taking. The kind they sell at Bruce Smith Drugs in Prairie Village. Then one day she got a passing score and our family doubled in size in three years. Money left my wallet and moths moved in.

The middle years. These years were a blur. The media would call us a SIMC—single income, multiple children. I had another acronym—SDBF—sleep-deprived baby factory. One day we had movers at our front door, and we traded the 66205 zip code to 66209. We needed more space and this home obliged.

It was a two-story. The roofline extended up for 25 feet. The decorations were elaborate and lengthy. They included those icicle lights, and neighbors put them up themselves. My neighbor across the cul-de-sac was one of those fix-it guys that every subdivision has. His name was Rob. Like that guy on "Extreme Makeover," who wears Puka shells and says "dude" a lot. This was the start of a new era—keeping up the Joneses with the triple threat—ladders, electricity and extension cords.

Home-fix-it-guy had one of those ladders that expands to 50 feet. Something with a rope and pulleys you buy at Home Depot on Father's Day. The kind with a bold lettering that says "WARNING—if your name is Keenan, you may die." When the day arrived for my decorations, he loaned it to me. The lights, per the directions, were to go along the edge of the roof. I headed up. The wind was blowing and the boss below making sure I did it right. Other things complicated this adventure, such as my sons opening windows while I'm separating the cloud cover and asking me questions, such as: "How old is Santa?" "How does his sleigh fly?" "Where do babies come from?"

The later years. This period started last year—actually on the day I arrived home to find my home glowing like Three Mile Island. Small planes were circling on final approach to my driveway. I half expected to see three men holding gifts looking for a manger. All these lights were hung when I was out of town. The work of the "lawn boy."

My wife knew that, for me, ladders present weight and balance issues.

"You work too hard to get on a ladder. Come inside, relax, it's all taken care of." She had a big smile. I was actually relieved. And then I asked the question only men seem to care about—"How much did it cost?"

She paused, grabbed my hand and said, "Less than your funeral. Don't worry about it. It's Christmas."

At that instant, the moths added a subdivision. A moment later I accepted it all.

So last week lawn boy made a return visit, our meter is setting land speed records, and the legacy of Clark Griswold remains intact in south Leawood. Who cares. It's Christmas.

Published December 2, 2006

My daughter: Santa's last true believer

About 10 years ago I was in the checkout line at the Prairie Village Hen House. At that time, our four children were under the age of 7. I had dropped them all into the shopping cart, and what happened next was like WWF on wheels.

Around the produce department they started to argue and by the time we reached checkout it had turned to a full-blown slugfest, with screams and cries for help.

An elderly woman in line behind me, observing my stage in life, smiled and said, "They will grow up so fast. Enjoy these times!"

I don't recall my reply—probably a roll of the eyes—but as we prepare for Christmas I understand now more than ever her wisdom.

Today three of those children are teenagers. The fourth, our daughter, is in fourth grade. She is 10.

My teenagers seem to care little for Santa Claus or Advent or the birth of Jesus, so long as my wife and I understand clearly what they want. They are too busy finding the next social gathering at Town Center Plaza or playing an online video game against someone from Hong Kong.

Which brings me to my daughter. She is the one in the family who is, as they say, a true believer.

She has a wish list for Santa. She reads the books, watches "A Charlie Brown Christmas" and lies in bed at night and prays that she has been "nice." Opening the Advent calendar is one of the highlights of her day.

And since we moved to a new address since last Christmas, she has one question: "Does Santa know where we live now?"

It's a magical, special time, for her and for us, that has no equivalent in the remaining 11 months of the year.

It's the sheer innocence of someone who believes that reindeer can fly around the world in 24 hours. A fourth-grader who doesn't flinch at the notion that an obese man who wears fake fur, employs elves and lives at the North Pole is someone we invite into our home while we sleep.

This girl admires our Nativity scene, rearranges the baby Jesus and cares about the ornament arrangements on the tree. She actually wants to go to church. Her radio station of choice is, of course, the "Christmas Music Station"—98.1.

Daughters this age—especially during Christmas—are what keep parents sane. She is the one child who shares secrets, talks about her day at school, draws for hours and then displays her work throughout the house. Her bedroom is clean and organized. Unlike her brothers' rooms, you can step in without stepping on yesterday's underwear, socks and shirt.

My wife and I now know these times are fleeting.

We know this Christmas will likely be the last time we prepare for a visitor from the North Pole, closing the door as parents to a time that we will always treasure but never revisit, and opening it to an entirely new set of issues, challenges and resolutions.

So on Christmas Eve, while her three brothers play the Xbox, our daughter will make the Santa cookies with her mom, go over her list one more time and then try to stay awake, listening for the faintest noise, the slightest hint that Santa has arrived. And 10 minutes later she will be sound asleep.

Originally published December 3, 2005.

New Year's Eve parties: Count me out

New Year's Eve, tradition tells us, is a night to celebrate. The media contributes to this, with television specials on that night, hosted by washed-up celebrities featuring washed-up entertainers who are desperate for exposure. Local promoters contribute to the hype, as they plan elaborate parties at places like Union Station.

This creates an expectation that my wife and I should party like we care that it's New Years Eve (NYE). But we don't. In my opinion, NYE is the most over hyped, overblown holiday of the year. The Y2K celebration was pretty much a dud, despite a thousand years to prepare. The world did not end, the power stayed on, and my computer crashed just as much as it did in 1999.

I can count at least six reasons why NYE is a bust.

Germs. Unless you just walked off a spaceship, you know the flu bug is killing men, women and children. The flu shot gives us some help, but they made 100 shots for 100 million people. I don't have one, and I don't know anyone who has one either. Yet one of the big traditions on New Year's is to kiss everyone when the clock strikes midnight. Call me strange, but this is not the year I want a sloppy kiss from some drunk 60-year-old with a bad cold sore. Based on my experience, these New Year kisses are not pecks on the cheeks. Rather, they tend to be the product of too much booze, too little discretion, and are lip-locking, teenage-inspired messes. No thanks.

Drunken drivers. New Year's is the only holiday that has as its main purpose to get liquored up and act foolish. And because these parties are rarely next door, you end up driving halfway across town to get in the action. I have zero interest being on the roads on the same night that some high school sophomore who just drank his first keg attempts to navigate Ward Parkway while calling his girlfriend on his cell phone. The newspapers are full of stories about safe drivers at the wrong end of some careless driver. No thanks.

Champagne. I have never liked this stuff and refuse to pretend it's good. It's got more bubbles than Diet Coke that's been dropped from a skyscraper. It has a sweet taste that does not mix well with the alcoholic bite. And it leaves you with a headache that lasts a month. No thanks.

Midnight. I'm too old to attend any party that is just getting started at midnight. By my calendar, Christmas was just six days ago, and between the eve and the next morning, I got about three hours of sleep that I've not regained in the interim. No thanks.

Baby sitters. It's impossible to find someone to watch our kids. If you don't know why, you obviously don't read my columns. And while my sons are normally old enough to get by without a sitter, New Year's presents certain issues that require adult supervision—like my sons' tendency to confuse NYE with the Fourth of July. No thanks.

Balloons. The big parties, like the one at Union Station tonight, is dropping balloons on the partygoers at midnight. As a general proposition, I am opposed to anything falling on my head late in the evening. Balloons, I suppose, are pretty harmless, until you realize that at Union Station they are dropping a couple thousand of them, which people then feel compelled to pop while guzzling champagne and kissing everyone in sight. No thanks.

So tonight we are staying home. Safe and sound. That's my idea to start off 2004 on the right note.

Published December 31, 2003.

An open letter to Santa Claus

Dear Santa Claus:

It's time for my annual letter. Let's start with things I'm tired of. Annoying Christmas cards from perfect families. Especially those dressed in matching everything. Posed in front of unusual locales, like Mount Everest, Fiji Island, the Eiffel tower, or Times Square. Somewhere out there is a family with a photo taken at Sears, where the baby is cross-eyed and the dad wears overalls. Where the backdrop is a bookshelf painted on plastic. I want to be the mailing list for that family. We are probably related.

Now for my needs. I need a tool. Let's start with a hammer. Not sure what I would do with it, maybe pound something. I need another screwdriver—the one I bought at Gomers liquor store—I drained over Thanksgiving.

I want my KU Jayhawks to go to a Bowl Game. I know, it's too late, but explain to me why Coach Mark Mangino did not get invited to the Papa Johns bowl. Or the Chick-Fil-A bowl. He was clearly "bowl eligible."

Santa, for some reason I keep growing in the wrong places. Places that shouldn't expand, like my neck. I've gone from a 15 neck size to a 16 ½ in three years, and buttons are busting out all over the place. Other things I've noticed. My eye bags are inflating. Wednesday morning I got up and stared at my face. It was spooky. I have hair turning up where it shouldn't be. I'm looking like you, basically. And then you have my feet. My wife says I need a pedicure and that it will require a team of assistants and an entire weekend. Apparently Wal-Mart offers these. She suggests I find one in Topeka or Wichita, where I will never be seen.

My high school senior needs a full ride to a college, any college, especially one that doesn't require a car. An added bonus would be one that has limited cell coverage so his phone bill is less than tuition.

Santa, my sons need an alarm clock. Something that dumps them out of bed, strips the sheets and starts the shower with a recording "Hot water almost gone!" A mood ring for my daughter that gives me a heads up on what to expect when I roll in from work.

I need more information about my high school sons. They claim I violate their privacy—a word that I don't recognize. Sharper Image has a device that tracks where your teenager drives and at what speed. The ads say it "secretly keep tabs on anything that moves." I need that. I found a book I want. "The Visual Guide to Lock Picking." It promises to teach you techniques "to pick most common locks, but also goes through what to do step-by-step; and actually teaches you how to do it." Call me interested.

Bernie the dog is my best friend. She never talks back and has never interrupted a family dinner with a text message. She needs her own bed because mine is getting crowded.

My wife has needs. A year's supply of Kleenex for when college boy heads out. Jewelry would be nice. Macy's has some things 75 percent off. Bring a coupon.

And if you deliver these wishes, you can get our men and women home from the Middle East soon. And that the peace on Earth thing? Let's swing that too.

Merry Christmas!

Published Christmas 2006.

9

Faith

My two brothers and two sisters never missed a single Sunday mass at St. Patrick's church in Great Bend. Neither snow nor rain nor gloom of night kept us from Sunday services. And when on vacation, we found a church, somewhere, someplace, and after services, my dad would introduce each and every one of us to the Pastor. And then, for good measure, my parents built the house where I was raised across the street from a Convent—yes, I said Convent. The Dominican Sisters of Great Bend. You can look it up.

First Confession Memorable

Like most parents, I take great joy watching my children trace the steps I walked as a child, whether in school, sports or life. And when those experiences converge with something so fundamental as your religious faith, it's a cause for both inspiration and humor. But if the event is your second-grade son experiencing his first "confession," there is more material than I can fit in five articles.

Confession, among Catholics, is what they call a Sacrament. That means it's a big deal—right up there with baptism, marriage and the rites that priests administer to people near death. It's special. And a couple years ago the Pope changed the name, and now it's termed "reconciliation." A kinder, gentler term, they say.

But semantics has done nothing to minimize the sheer terror it brings to a 7-year-old spilling his guts to a 62-year-old priest. A boy whose only frame of reference in the sin department is the Ten Commandments, which means he must figure out if he has committed "adultery."

In 1967, in Great Bend, Kan., it truly was "confession." You dropped to your knees before Father Zimmer and spilled your guts like a criminal suspect on

"NYPD Blue." You held nothing back from Father Zimmer. He rarely smiled. He even spoke a different language when he said Mass. So there was nothing fun about rattling off your sins while kneeling in a dark, crowded booth, with only a paper-thin wire mesh separating you from virtually God himself.

Back then, life was different. Dads spanked. Heck, moms spanked. We went to church every day, and our parents expected us to be priests. It was "The Wonder Years" meets the Vatican. Then, like now, in the eyes of a second-grader, reconciliation is still confession. And confession is still scary.

On Robert's recent big day, we made the trek to church. The drive seemed longer than usual. He was quiet. Dressed. You could see his brain churning, thinking of what to say. We entered and took our seat. For the first time in his life, he did not use the pew as a bed, a fort or couch. He knelt down, closed his eyes and (could it be?) prayed.

His brothers marveled at the scene, like they were old pros watching a rookie hit a grand slam. Sure, they had prepped their kid brother, providing him with a degree of comfort, as brothers do, while adding their own "checklist" of sorts of topics to cover:

1. Disobeying dad.
2. Being mean to his younger sister.
3. Talking back to dad.

Then to buy time, repeat 1-3.

I'm told, reliably, that hearing the confession of a 7-year-old varies considerably, depending on many factors, including the influence of siblings and the gender of the confessor. Seven-year-old daughters, as a general matter, come clean and spare no details. They talk about hurting others' feelings and being disrespectful. They speak softly and with great remorse. Tears flow freely. Their visit runs about five minutes. Sons, on the other hand, cram it in about 45 seconds, and tell a much different story that goes something like this: "I yelled twice. I disobeyed three times and was bad a couple other times. But my brother has been worse. He even cussed one time—in church—while you were talking. His name is Tommy."

Little Robert pulled it off, however. He walked toward the priest, turned to make eye contact with his mother, then sat down to tell his story. About a minute later, a true religious sacrament was experienced: Every sin ever committed was forgiven—wiped clean.

As he finished reciting his checklist and turned to rejoin his parents, a smile crossed his lips. A grin bigger than any goal ever scored, any baseball ever hit, any point ever tallied. And for that brief time, I would swear you could see the shadow of a halo form above his head. And then, almost instantly, it seemed to vanish. But for at least that one passing moment, he secured his spot inside the Pearly Gates.

A true miracle.

Published March 3, 2001

My daughter's first communion: rehearsing for the wedding

It's the first of May, and for Catholic second grade boys and girls that means one thing: First Communion.

A Sacrament that like its counterpart, First Confession, welcomes 8- and 9-year-olds into the central fabric of the Catholic faith. In our home, for my only daughter, this occasion is huge. It's like a bat mitzvah without a DJ, prom without a boyfriend. And for this weekend, nothing else matters.

This occasion has strong secular traditions. Clothes top the list. For the boys, a blue sport coat, clip-on tie and scuffed-up shoes is pretty standard fare—all purchased the prior week at Wal-Mart.

In our home, my third son earned the right to wear exactly what his brothers wore years earlier. His belt was wrapped around his skinny waist and pulled tight. His hair was soaked in massive quantities of gel guaranteed to suppress pop-ups for at least two hours. We snapped a roll of film, tossed it in a drawer and I'm not certain we even had it developed.

For girls it's much different. It's like a wedding. Only more expensive. Both are Sacraments. Both are once-in-a-lifetime events. Both include an elaborate walk down the church aisle. Both require sparkling white dresses, veils, gloves and shoes, all preserved in airtight bags and stored in King Tut's tomb for generations to wear.

The trappings often include a white prayer book (never opened), shoulder bag, handmade rosary and special socks with 18 layers of lace. In the old days, the accessories included something we called a "scapular" (like a medal only bigger) which Sister Mary Rose told me that if you wore it when you died, you got a speeding ticket on the way to heaven.

Mine lasted about two days.

But there is at least one important difference from a wedding. On this day, your daughter doesn't share the limelight with a clumsy groom. Or his annoying mom who thinks she is in charge.

A day this big has other complications, however.

Like locating the baptismal certificate, which in the Catholic church is more valuable than a birth certificate and passport combined.

Everyone wants the perfect photograph while the little angel strolls toward the altar. This has prompted soccer moms to act like teenagers at a Backstreet Boys concert, brushing aside half the congregation while they use enough flash bulbs to prompt a rolling blackout.

Our church now explains the rules very clearly. One professional photographer. One individual photograph. Remain calm. Exhale.

But nothing compares to the class portrait. If a picture is worth a thousand words, then these photographs contain enough statements to fill an Encyclopedia Britannica. It's the only photograph of 65 children where everyone actually stands still and smiles on cue.

The beauty of this Kodak moment is capturing everyone whose appearance is more preposterous than your own child. Those boys with four, not two older brothers, for example. Or those girls whose veils obscure three rows of boys behind them.

My dad's picture some 60 years ago is something out of Angela's Ashes. Mine, a still shot from St. Patrick's parish, Great Bend, circa 1969, is remarkable for the glow surrounding my head. On that day, mom reserved my spot at the seminary in nearby Victoria.

She cancelled it 12 hours later.

So today, my sons better get out of the way and shut up. They had their day, and if it wasn't memorable, it's their fault. They are boys.

And for the residents of the rest of the city, I suggest avoiding all interactions with my wife, who tends to deal poorly with stress of this magnitude. Avoid our home, our subdivision and probably Leawood completely. Play it safe and take a day trip to Topeka.

At 2 p.m., the clouds will part, the sun will shine, the birds will sing in harmony, the lion shall lay down with the lamb, and at Nativity Parish, for one precious 9-year-old, life will be divine.

May 1, 2004.

Christmas Plays and Holiday Concerts—calling all teacher pets!

The holiday season is a festive time. And no place gets into the mood more than the Catholic schools, where this takes on life in two ways: the Christmas musical and the school play. Here is my take on these timeless classics.

School Christmas Concert. This event takes months of planning and weeks of rehearsals and involves every child, K-8. Super Bowls are less of a production. There is not enough booze on the planet to get me to pull this off. That's why there is a special place reserved in heaven for all music directors. Most of whom, due to work stress, arrive there prematurely.

Our school holds these in the church, which is quite large. But by the time parents, grandparents, uncles, aunts, siblings, toddlers pile it, it has the intimacy of a crammed phone booth. This prompts some parents to reserve half the church for their late arriving third cousins. They spread coats, sweaters, blankets over entire pews and then guard the turf. After all, the holiday spirit only goes so far when it comes to protecting those front row seats. I've heard that some innovative Pastors auction off the prime seats to these functions. I'm happy to watch from the vestibule where you can hear nothing and see even less.

Another sure thing are the students' fashion statements. When daughters are no longer constrained by a school uniform policy, they take full advantage. They dress like a BOTAR rehearsal. Accessories abound. They smile broadly and represent all that is good about Christmas. The boys, on the other hand, wear whatever the mom grabbed off the bedroom floor. Their ties are drawn tight, reducing blood flow to their brain. They are miserable and have no interest hiding their true feelings. At some point in the concert, someone will either faint or barf during "Jingle Bells." All preserved on hundreds of video cameras that no one will ever watch.

By mid December, the flu and cold season is in overdrive. Consequently, these functions offer a buffet of germs yet unknown to the world's best drug companies. By the final song, everyone is sick. They just don't know it yet.

We did all this in St. Pats, circa 1972. Except I have no memory of these events becoming family reunions. So I asked my dad about this over Thanksgiving. He said back then dads worked to make a living and didn't have time for such nonsense. He also admitted that he was probably at the Knight of Columbus mingling with his fellow parishioners celebrating the holiday season as great Catholic men used to do.

Christmas Pageant. These things are generally shorter than the concerts and tend to be reserved for the younger grades. The live nativity scenes used to be really popular when I was at St. Pats. Joseph and Mary were the choice roles. The teachers' pets' got these roles. These were the perennial suck ups who brought treats to the teachers on every imaginable occasion. Next to those coveted spots, you had the Three Wise Men. These were the second tier of brown noses who sat on the front row of daily church and pretended to pray the entire mass. I could be found in the back row trading punches with Marty Murphy. Maybe that explains why I was the donkey and Marty was the hay bale. Back then the joke was that Hays—our rival city to the north—could never have a live nativity scene because they lacked Three Wise Men and a virgin. (OK its old but still a classic)

So it is the most wonderful time of the year. And if your holiday routine includes a Christmas concert, I recommend a stiff martini to help you enjoy the night.

December, 2004

10

My Parents, Ramona and Larry

My parents' devotion to each other was second only to their devotion to their five children. I was the middle-born. Two older—Kate and Tim, and two younger—Marty and Beth. My best stories are those about Mona and Larry.

Father's Day brings memories of mother

In my 43 years of life, I have seen my father cry twice. The first time was 16 years ago, when he tried to explain to me why he couldn't deliver the eulogy for his second-closest friend. The other time was last month, at the funeral of his best friend. His wife of 49 years. My mother.

Mom was special, as all moms by their nature are special. Even though tomorrow is Father's Day, this column is about my mother.

Mom died on Memorial Day, the day after she decorated the graves of friends who had no relatives in the city where she lived, Great Bend, Kan. She wanted her late friends to have something meaningful adorn their grave sites.

That was my mom. She was like many mothers, always more concerned with everyone else's problems and offering to help. She was an interested listener, a warm pair of hands, a bright smile, a prolific letter writer to all her five children. That was Mom.

My mom was the only daughter of Jacob and Olga Goering, the two truest Germans you could ever meet. She had only one sibling. The Goerings were Mennonites and lived in town called Kingman, west of Wichita. As a kid, I knew they were special. They wore hats and bonnets and always served ice water at church and family functions. They were deeply dedicated to their faith. My dad is Irish Catholic. He had eleven brothers and sisters. His religious traditions also ran deep. His family gatherings were always a bit more, well, spirited. By any conventional standards, it was a marriage that posed many challenges.

Both my parents were products of a great generation—born in the '20s and '30s, married in the '50s. Marriages formed in these years grew stronger, not weaker, in the face of adversity. Obstacles were merely opportunities. Almost all of my parents' friends today enjoy long marriages. It was a time when faith was the central building block for everything else in life—when priorities started, and finished, with family.

On Memorial Day, when mom suddenly fell ill, she reminded my dad about her funeral file. Dad brushed it off, of course, hopeful that this woman who had enjoyed 72 years of almost perfect health would recover quickly. She used to joke about the file in which she planned her own funeral. Mom was an organist at church and had assisted at probably a hundred funerals. She had strong views about her own funeral: the music, the Scriptures, the burial. On Monday evening, my two brothers located the file. Neatly organized, it was brimming with notes, funeral cards and obituaries of friends who had passed over the years.

At the bottom of a manila envelope was a small piece of paper. It was no bigger than a paper clip and went undetected by my brothers when they first went through the file. When I retrieved and read it, I knew it captured everything about my mom, and probably yours as well:

"Our mother laughed our laughter, shed our tears, returned our love, feared our fears. She lived our joys, cared our cares. And all our hopes and dreams she shared."

Ramona Jean Keenan. My mother.

Published June 15, 2002

Mother's devotion endures in memories and letters

On this Mother's Day weekend I've decided to write about my mom, Ramona Jean Keenan. But mom will never read this column. She died three years ago this month, abruptly, after 72 years of life. I think about mom from time to time, though with the passage of time I think about her less and less. I feel guilty about that and wonder if my children will ever forget about me. But about every couple weeks her memory comes to mind. Sometimes out of the blue. Sometimes I will stumble across one of her old letters, most of which I have kept.

Mom wrote all five of her children letters almost weekly. Usually they were group letters, addressed "Dear Children." Others she wrote to us individually. All were typed on an old-fashioned typewriter. Mom's letters were part inspiration, part celebration, and all love. She signed every one: "Loving you, Mother."

When I find one, I read it and cry. Like most moms, our problems were her problems. As the saying goes, she was only as happy as her unhappiest child.

My mom was no better than yours, of course. But she was more fortunate than many moms, in some ways. She never sent any of her sons to Vietnam, and never had to attend any funerals of her children. None of my siblings had any drug or alcohol problems, though my oldest sister was the poster child of "experimentation."

Mom lived a life free of cancer, arthritis and most other medical conditions that come with aging. Mom had a great partner for 49 years of it all, dad.

All in all, not a bad life, I suppose.

But one of my mom's strengths was her ability to build bridges. You see, mom was raised in a strict Mennonite family—German Mennonite. Her parents were Olga and Jacob Goering. Dad was Irish Catholic. Mom had one sibling. Dad had 11. The Goerings didn't tolerate alcohol and never thought much of the Pope.

The Keenans had a fondness for both. In 1952 "The Church" wasn't very hospitable to non-converts. One day I asked mom why her wedding photo was taken in the church vestibule. She explained that back then non-Catholics were not allowed to marry inside the church. I then asked why there were no photos of her parents at the wedding. They did not attend, she admitted very sheepishly, because of "religion issues."

Mom later became Catholic and for 30 some years was the church organist at St. Pats in Great Bend, Kan. Dad befriended Jake and Olga and over time hard feelings softened. Dad eventually won them over, and they even traveled to the "homeland" together (Germany, not Ireland—dad knew his limits!). Yet through it all my parents' love for one another—and their dedication to their children, their parents, their friends—endured, prospered, flourished.

But what I remember more than anything else about mom was an expression she had. When mothers speak directly to their children they pack a lot of emotion. Mom had a phrase that embodied the nurturing and caring of all moms.

The first time she spoke these words I was leaving for college. I heard it almost every time I left home from that point on. It was 1977 when Mom hugged me, held me, and looked me in the eyes. What she said I will always remember: "You're very important to me."

And so this week something happened that made me think of mom again. I had a dream Sunday night about mom. There was much that didn't make sense to me in the dream. She was dropping me off in the car at a place that was not familiar to me. It was strange but seemed so real.

And just before she left me, she hugged me and said, "You're very important to me."

Ramona Jean Keenan. My mom.

Published May 7, 2005.

In the basement, without their Rock

The Wizard of Oz" made Kansas synonymous with tornadoes. But it took the Topeka tornado of June 1966 to bring this Hollywood fiction to reality. That twister was, at the time, said to be the most costly tornado in our country's history.

Even though I grew up three hours west of Topeka in Great Bend, that event had a dramatic effect on my life, particularly during the tornado season. Tornado drills, which were infrequent rituals, became mandatory in schools and brought a new set of do's and don'ts to those of us in the hinterlands. One of the most important rules, repeated endlessly, was never, ever attempt to outdrive any twister. In fact, the rules included the directive to stop driving and crawl in the nearest ditch.

This order was on par with other truisms, like avoiding windows and invoking the Lord's name in vain.

So in the years after the Topeka twister, spring always carried with it the fear that it was Great Bend's turn for the big one. The one calming influence in this was my dad. He was, like most dads in the 1950s and '60s, a model of composure.

Always under control. Always in command.

And so in May 1969 when a huge twister hit the ground a couple of miles west of Great Bend, it appeared our day had arrived to join Dorothy and Toto. Our home—a brick bomb shelter—was nevertheless directly in its path. My mom and my four siblings huddled with me in the basement, each of us doing 30 laps around the beads.

But our Rock was missing. He was on his way home from the office.
Suddenly the front door flew open. Dad came flying down the stairs screaming at the top of his lungs.

"Everyone in the car. We've got to get out of here!"
It was the most outrageous thing I had ever heard in 10 years of life. From the Rock, no less. My older sister went from quiet sobs to screaming, "I'm too young to die!" Mom, of course, didn't question the Rock. She gathered us up. Out we went and into the Chrysler Station Wagon—the model with plastic wood paneling.

Dad hit the gas. We were plastered to the back of the vinyl seats.

"This is our only hope," he said.
The roads were empty. No cars, no people, no nothing.
Dad started running stop signs and red lights, and when he turned on the radio, the first thing we heard brought utter silence to the car:
"Whatever you do, do not, I repeat, DO NOT get in your car and attempt to outdrive the tornado."

No one said a word.

The twister changed its path and spared the entire city. And we got home, piled out of the car and scattered throughout the house. My brothers and sisters pretended nothing ever happened.

Published Fathers Day, 2006

Remembering the father of all fish stories

I always assumed my dad was like most other dads. Or at least it seemed so growing up. Back then, all my friends' dads spanked when circumstances required it. Dad reserved it for rare occasions, of course. Like when my brothers fought, which was a lot, actually. Or the day my teenage sister used the f-word in a fit of rage. On that afternoon in July, dad skipped the paddle and went straight to the belt. Mom stood by and never flinched. There was a lesson to be taught, and he was one very impressive teacher. Dad had a couple other rules, no different than the other parents I knew. That Sundays meant church and church clothes. That you got a job at age 16. And life guarding and caddying were not jobs.

Larry Keenan was one of 12 children, and he lost his mother at age 11. That experience shaped the kind of father he was in raising my two brothers and two sisters.

Dad showed us that marriages were for life. That friendships meant couples stopping by without any formal invitation and sitting in the kitchen for hours while my dad "fixed them a drink." Dad also showed us that measuring my sisters' skirts from the knees was the only objective way to dictate good taste. He was a testament to the importance of prayers at night, which he led in the hallway outside our bedrooms. He could say a Hail Mary and Our Father in less than 15 seconds and make us feel good about it. And his love of polyester knee socks remains his most important fashion statement.

Family vacations meant Colorado. Dad never used cruise control for some reason; I guess that would restrict his God-given right to constantly speed up and slow down for the entire trip. And the road consisted of the lane, the shoulder and substantial portions of the ditch.

But perhaps no single event defined the dad's role in my life than one day in the early '70s. My brothers and I brought home a huge fish that we wanted cleaned. I was probably 10 at the time. We caught all kinds of fish back then. But this was more than any fish. This was a carp. You see, no one ever cleans a carp because no one ever keeps a carp, the worst looking, worst tasting fish God ever put on this planet.

But on this day, my dad, caught up with the moment, labored over that fish for at least an hour, cutting, pulling, dissecting those parts worth eating and those not. The heat was bad, and the flies were worse. And when he finished the task, he looked up, sweat pouring down his brow and uttered words that still ring in my head. "Next time you catch one of these, *throw the darn thing back*." And what my brother said shook my dad to his core: "*Dad, we didn't catch it*." he said. "*Some man caught it and gave it to us*."

What happened next was a blur. I know he borrowed heavily from my sister's vocabulary. I do know, however, that the fish—what was left of it—never made it to the freezer.

In more recent years, dad's daily routine includes spending every morning reading the obituaries, looking for the names of friends, relatives, clients—and maintaining mom's gravesite.

So on this upcoming Father's Day, I remember something that Theodore Hesburgh, president emeritus of Notre Dame, once said about what makes a good father. Something that fits for my dad, and perhaps yours as well: "The most important thing a father can do for his children is to love their mother." *Happy Father's Day.*

Published June 16, 2004.

Looking past loss to embrace love

At some point in life all of us come to accept the mortality of our parents. For some, it comes at a young age. My dad was 11 when his mother died of cancer. I was more fortunate. My mother lived to be 72.

And however difficult the loss to a son or daughter, the spousal pain is magnified tenfold. Widowers have more difficulty "coping." My dad—like many men of his generation—was incredibly dependent on Mom. They were life partners, soul mates, pick your cliché. And shortly after mom's death it became clear my dad's own life expectancy was becoming diminished.

In contrast, widows find a way to adapt, cope, move on. Case in point—my mother-in-law. Her husband died 10 years ago of a brain tumor. Since then, Lee never looked back. She belongs to eight different bridge clubs, stays active and is the world's finest babysitter. My wife tells me she still mourns, and I'm sure she does, but it's hard to see it through the smile she wears every day. So these contrasts have hit our home hard, and brought to mind the expression, "When there is a death in a marriage, women mourn, men replace."

It raises an important difference about the sexes, and can be a flashpoint between sons and daughters of a widower. Women want romance, hugging, candlelight dinners. Men need someone to organize their world, complement their social lives and keep them company. Or, as my wife says, someone to "cook, clean and pick up after them."

All this intrigued me. I found where the Census Bureau estimates that 10 times as many widowers as widows older than 65 remarry, though there are fewer older men than older women.

Like most men in their 70s, my dad has many friends. And one of those friends was a widow named Patti, a longtime family friend whose husband, Bud, died in a plane accident 16 years earlier. Bud and dad were best friends. The day of Bud's funeral in 1986 was the first time I had seen my father cry.

In the months after his death, Patti dedicated her life to raising her four children, now all medical doctors. Then she spent the rest of her time helping others. She operates at one speed—fast.

So when Patti stepped in to help dad, it came with some resistance from my sisters, and some of my mom's friends. There was opposition, and at times it was not very cordial. But over time, my two sisters came to accept that our father deserved from his five children what he spent a lifetime giving us—unconditional love.

And then one day it happened. Dad called me. He had something on his mind. And I said, "Dad, do what makes you happy. It's your life. You have to live it. Whatever you decide, we will support you."

And two weeks later I had a letter in the mail. And this is what it said: "To my children: You know that I loved your mother more than I can express. I love her now and will always love her. And, I'm sure that because of her, I do not like being alone. At this point, I am nearly 75 years old and if I am going to make a change in my life, I need to do it now." Dad explained that he was engaged to Patti, with a wedding date six weeks away. "I have prayed about my life and what I should do. I am sure this is the right decision and that your mother agrees with it." I cried then. I cry now.

So two years ago this month, on a beautiful fall day, we loaded up the Suburban and drove to Wichita. To attend a wedding of two adults who between them had celebrated 83 years of marriage to someone else. Officiated by a priest whom I saw last at my mother's funeral. Everyone there thought of two people who were missing. It was, at times, very sad. But through it all, there was also joy and happiness.

And it has continued.

So I dedicate this column to all those who, like Dad and Patti, found love after loss. And to those sons and daughters who can blink away the tears and tell them, "It's OK."

Published September, 2006.

978-0-595-43851-8
0-595-43851-2

Printed in the United States
110421LV00002B/112-204/A